Praise For *Moments Matter* And Dave Sanderson

"In a time when people are looking for leaders to motivate and inspire them, Dave's message is filled with inspiration and courage. His story is an example of how doing what's right can transform your life. In *Moments Matter* Dave shares the 12 Resources he used to survive 'The Miracle on the Hudson' plane crash. These valuable Resources and the remarkable stories he shares will impact everyone who reads this book."

– Rep. Brian Brown, North Carolina House of Representatives

"Dave Sanderson's incredibly moving story reminds us that it is from ordinary circumstances that extraordinary events occur. We are all made better if we heed his lesson: no matter where we are, we must be ready and we must anticipate, because Moments Matter."

– `Trip Durham, College Sports Announcer Duke University / Founder, 2D Consulting, LLC

"The physicians, nurses and staff of Palisades Medical Center have a strong connection to 'The Miracle on the Hudson.' Our staff took great pride in caring for Dave Sanderson and several other passengers following the plane's emergency landing. Dave has remained a true friend and supporter of Palisades Medical Center by staying in close contact with many of our employees. Dave's experiences and life lessons have made a powerful impact on our staff, and I am sure *Moments Matter* will truly inspire and motivate all readers."

– Bruce J. Markowitz, President & CEO, Palisades Medical Center

"Many believe they'll never need the Red Cross, just like Dave did before that fateful morning. Dave Sanderson's powerful account of how the Red Cross touched him three times within 24 hours and willingness to share his story means we'll continue to be there for our neighbors during their neediest hour."

– Kay W. Wilkins, Louisiana Regional Chief Executive of
the American Red Cross

"Some of us are put into situations for a reason – we don't know when, why, or what will happen. Dave was chosen and his story is truly one that consists of leadership, motivation and inspiration."

– Henry P. Cortacans, MAS, CEM, NREMT-P, State Planner, Emergency
Medical Services Task Force, State of New Jersey

"It is extremely rare after a plane crash for first responders to find survivors. Dave Sanderson is one of those lucky people who has lived to share his personal story of survival and how his inner voice of reason helped him save not only himself but many others! I am humbled to be in his circle of friends! People like Dave make putting my life on line well worth the risk."

– Captain/Paramedic Stacy Gerlich, Los Angeles Fire Department,
Los Angeles Operational Area. Homeland Security Division

"Dave Sanderson is a man whose faith has been tested in an extreme crisis. God has given him the gift and passion to connect his experience with the lives of countless individuals across the world. I am grateful for his witness, and for the encouragement and wisdom he offers in these pages."

– Ken Carter, Resident Bishop, Florida Area United Methodist Church

"I was Director Emergency Planning & Response for US Airways when flight 1549 made an emergency landing on the Hudson River. I have heard Dave tell about his and his fellow passengers compelling experience. The skillful landing and safe evacuation of everyone is truly unforgettable."

– Deborah Thompson, President Deborah Thompson & Associates Inc.,
former Emergency Response Manager for US Airways

"*Moments Matter* speaks to everyone. Perspective, people and preparation are the keys to success in life and business. Dave's genuine and sincere approach is refreshing."

– Gary A. Scott, President, Real Estate Brokerage,
Long and Foster Companies, Inc.

"Dave has taken an absolutely terrifying life experience on US Air flight #1549, 'The Miracle on the Hudson,' that tested his faith, as well as his personal abilities, and created a teaching tool for all in life lessons. His selfless actions during that day saved lives and Dave continues to do that by sharing his story and the importance of anticipation, teamwork, leadership and creating your own flight plan. He continues to inspire leaders from all walks worldwide and this book is a must read!!"

– Mr. Dana J. Bradley, Performance Holdings, Principal,
Entrepreneurs' Org, Member leader, Charlotte, NC

"Dave Sanderson captivates audiences with his personal and authentic story. As he walks you through what happened that day on the Hudson, you feel like you are right there with him. Dave's message makes you think about how you personally would have handled the situation and how it would affect who you are today. His message reminds us to be our best every day and to live life to its fullest. Everyone should hear Dave's story. It's a universal message that leaves a lasting impression!"

— Angela Cox-Weston, Midwest Speakers Bureau, Inc

"Dave Sanderson serves as an inspirational guide on how to manage your mental state to focus on doing the right thing in business and in life. The practical insights found in his message will help you become a better leader and build a much stronger team - prepared to face any obstacle."

— Joey Davenport, CLU, CLF, President, Hoopis Performance Network

"Before the miracle of US AIRWAYS flight 1549, I reported directly to Dave Sanderson as part of an International Security Detail, for more than a decade. Dave's ability to galvanize personalities toward the objective of providing a safe environment within a hostile atmosphere were unparalleled. His ability to lead our team at critical junctures, in an environment of stress and uncertainty created the evolution of a passionate team of exceptional performers. It isn't surprising that Dave was a huge contributor to the rescue efforts that fateful day."

— Michael Melio, President Western Piedmont Metal, Inc. and Entrepreneur

"Dave Sanderson's appreciation for life after what he experienced... is infectious. His inspirational words and story transcend to people of all ages. Being in the TV business, I've interviewed many wonderful speakers... but none as memorable as Dave."

– Alex Delgado, "Central Valley Today" Talk Show Host
Fresno, California

"Jarring danger can either intimidate and immobilize, or inspire action and lasting reflection about what is essential. The latter is what Dave Sanderson embodies - with graciousness under pressure, generosity of spirit and in deed, and above all, inspiring faith."

– Ulrike K. Hood, Montblanc Charlotte, North Carolina

"Between events occurring in our lives and how we respond to them there is a space. There we make some of life's most important choices all too often in only an instant. Learning to make the best choices in those spaces is inside *Moments Matter*."

– Dr. Brad Roof, Hantzmon Wiebel Faculty Scholar,
James Madison University

"Life isn't a matter of milestones,

but of moments."

–Rose Kennedy

DEDICATION

Moments Matter is dedicated to my wife, Terri, and my children, Chelsey, Colleen, Courtney, and Chance. You are the five most important people in my life, and I love you more than I can ever say in words.

This book is also dedicated to Tony Robbins and my security team from the Anthony Robbins Companies. We spent many days and nights together focusing on a common mission and you held me to a higher standard which inspired me to "make the move" to live my dream to help others realize their potential.

What are you
grateful for today?

"Gratitude can transform common days into
thanksgivings, turn routine jobs into joy, and change
ordinary opportunities into blessings."
–William Arthur Ward

CONTENTS

"We've had a miracle on 34th Street.
I believe now we've had a miracle on the
Hudson. This is a potential tragedy that may have
become one of the most magnificent days in the
history of New York City agencies."
–David Paterson, Governor of New York

FOREWORD

Mike Maddock
CEO and Founding Partner, Maddock Douglas, Inc.

**"Life has a way of offering us valuable lessons if
we are paying attention."
–Mike Maddock**

A couple of years ago, my wife Ruthie walked into the kitchen and said, "Well, I did it, I outlived my mom today." I was a bit stunned by the statement but not by the fact. I was very aware that her mom had died very suddenly when she was in high school, an event that changed her life forever and something she has reflected upon every single day of her life. It was no small wonder that Ruth knew the exact time and date that her mom passed. No date on the calendar was more significant to her.

As I write this, our oldest son is sixteen — the same age Ruthie was when she lost her mom.

Life has a way of offering us valuable lessons if we are paying attention, which is why Ruthie's mom's death has been such a blessing to our family. Her passing has helped us to understand that every day is a gift and time is the most valuable thing that we have. Because of this, we have never put off a family vacation because of age, money, weather, or any other of the hundreds of reasons we could have used to wait "until the timing was just right." We've never put off a tough conversation. We say "I love you" every time we say goodbye to each other. Thankfully, our kids still say these words back to us.

We've learned to value the rain as much as the sunshine and the bad times as much as the good.

I suppose plane crashes would have a similar effect on a family.

When I heard Dave's recounting of his landing in the Hudson River, I saw that a similar realization was alive in him. His message is about his own deeply held values that were solidified forever on that fateful day. Thankfully, these values are now a treasure that he freely shares with leaders around the world. I was so impressed with the tenets that he espoused when I first heard him speak, that I invited him to a gathering of entrepreneurs at MIT's Endicott House. I wanted them to know what Ruthie and Dave think about constantly: every day, every moment on this planet is a gift to be treasured.

Leaders often think they can control the future. Mike Tyson famously said, "Strategy is great until you get punched in the face." This seems to be a modern day reworking of the old Yiddish truism, "We plan, God laughs." Whenever I find myself counting on, or trying to control future events, I am reminded of these words and Dave's great lessons. Dave has managed to use what others may see as the worst day of their lives to help clarify what made it one of his best, and he does it with candor, humility, and a sense of humor that is refreshing. And his words about how leaders make the most of the time they are given is one of life's important lessons.

So, how's your day going? There is a lesson here for us all.

A NOTE FROM THE AUTHORS

"You don't get the same moment
twice in life."
–Anon

Proximity is Power – Dave Sanderson

When I was young, my father taught me that it's important to have access to people who can help you achieve what you need and want in life. I was pretty sheltered where I grew up. The towns in which I grew up (Hillsboro, Ohio and Winchester, Virginia) were small, and everyone knew one another, so it was difficult to get into trouble. However, when I went to James Madison University, I discovered another world that included many different types of people. I tried to keep up with their lifestyles and either forgot or didn't want to pay attention to what I learned from my dad. This was a hard lesson for me to learn, but it has paid off in a number of different ways.

After college I worked in hotel restaurant management in Charlotte, North Carolina. I was the second assistant manager, which meant that I worked every night and weekend. This was a great learning experience for me, but one experience resonated with me and reinforced what my dad once told me. Every day, a gentleman would visit the restaurant to have a coffee and read the paper. I struck up a relationship with Bill. He was older (probably in his 60s), wore a flannel shirt, and drove a pickup truck. As the second assistant manager, I was required to work holidays. Around Christmas, Bill visited the restaurant. He asked me to come with him to the parking lot to see the present he planned to give his wife: a blue Corvette. Though I never asked Bill what he did for a living, I discovered that he owned 80 movie theaters throughout the Carolinas. He was one of the most successful business people in the Charlotte area. He asked me to drive the Corvette. He told me to point it in the right direction because it would take off quickly. We went for a test drive. He told me that I needed one of these vehicles. Unfortunately, I couldn't afford it, but he said that one day I would. He became my mentor. One of the lessons he taught me over the years was to always have access to and be around people I wanted to emulate—the same lesson that my father taught me when I was young. Bill, my mentor, passed away about three years ago, but I have never forgotten him or the lessons he taught me.

I first met Cindy Wrightson in 1999 when I was the assistant security director for Tony Robbins. She was in the Creative Department, and I was managing the team's operations. We traveled with Tony around the world and became close friends. I trusted Cindy and shared many things with her about my life. We had a lot of fun, though we worked long and unusual hours. When you work with someone so closely, you learn a lot about his or her character and values. We were both going through "stuff" in our real lives, which allowed us to relate to one another in terms of our experiences. In 2008, Cindy left the Robbins organization when I was Tony's security director. This position required more responsibility from me, but it was a great learning experience. Then, the incident known as the "Miracle on the Hudson" occurred, and everything in my life changed. I still worked for Oracle and acted as Tony's security director, but I was inundated with requests to speak to the media. Tony was tremendous during that time. He was the only one to reach out to me on the night of the "Miracle" and coached me on interacting with the media. One of the lessons I learned from Tony was "proximity is power," and I was able to realize this fact by being around him. This lesson was similar to the lesson my dad and Bill taught me about access. In February 2009, he held his Unleash the Power Within event in Secaucus, New Jersey. I told Tony that I would be there, but because the event was in New Jersey—only a few miles from the epicenter of where everything took place—I figured that some members of the media would show up. I was right. I was probably not at my best during that event, but I quickly realized that what Tony had told me for many years was true: it was time to work for myself and to influence others. About a year later, Tony and I spoke. I told him that I was making this transition. He was excited and supported me, though this meant that I was no longer able to be his security director. I hold Tony in the highest regard and am honored to call him my mentor and friend.

I kept in touch with Cindy as this was going on. I had an executive assistant, Tammy, who helped me establish my business. In addition, I had the support of Vickie and Lisa on my team who helped me refine my business. I then approached Cindy to see if she would help me bring my business content together. She cheerfully said yes. While I was working with Vickie about two years ago, she told me that I needed to identify all the events that occurred during that day of "The Miracle" as a record for my family. We spent about 9 to 10 hours recording this information, as well as collecting the resources that I used that day, to enable individuals to not only survive a plane crash, but to also thrive afterwards. We realized that the 12 different resources that I used on the plane that day were applicable to entrepreneurs or businesses. These resources were also applicable in the sense that they allowed individuals to survive immediate challenges to help them create something positive. I spoke with Cindy, and we decided that we should write a book to share this information with others.

Cindy was not only open to this challenge but was also excited for the opportunity. She is a master of taking disparate content and putting it together in such a way that anyone can relate to it. She performed this type of work for Tony Robbins for 10 years and was a key figure in his business, allowing him to influence millions of people. I could not have found a more suitable individual with a similar set of values to join me on this adventure. She has kept me strong. She has also taught me how to take life experiences and use them to help others.

Cindy and I named this book *Moments Matter* because everyone makes choices at each moment of every day. Each choice that we make is based on our values, skills, and the primary needs that drive us in any particular moment. The choices that I made on January 15, 2009 determined my destiny in the same way that certain choices influenced Captain Sullenberger, four crewmembers, and 149 other passengers. The next time you are in a crisis, which I will call your "personal plane crash," make a choice based on your personal values, skills, and primary needs. In addition to having a greater chance for survival, you will also grow.

I have been blessed to always have had access to people who can make an impact. The lessons that my father taught me when I was young and those that were reinforced by Bill when I was 23 were true. In addition, the lessons that Tony taught me were true. Having access and proximity should be cherished. My access to Cindy is a blessing, and I am truly honored that she has helped me with *Moments Matter*.

I hope you enjoy reading *Moments Matter* and can relate to and use some of the strategies. This way, the next time you face a "personal plane crash," you will realize that all of the moments in your life matter.

Be Where It Matters – Cindy Wrightson

Dave and I first met in 1999, a few months after I started working for Tony Robbins. For the next 10 years, I worked in the Creative Department of The Anthony Robbins Companies and often traveled around the world to support Tony and his various seminars. During that time, Dave and I became very good friends. Because of the nature of our jobs, we both worked in close proximity to Tony. As Dave was on Tony's security team, our paths crossed at events, often in the green room behind the stage or while waiting outside Tony's hotel suite to head to a venue. It was during these times that we shared important moments in our lives: In San Jose, I learned that Dave's wife, Terri, was pregnant with their son; in Orlando, we talked about my divorce; and while we were in Kona, Hawaii, in 2001, the 9/11 attacks occurred. In addition to a long friendship, we share a deep sense of faith, a loyalty to family and friends, a strong work ethic, and a profound respect and appreciation for Tony Robbins and the lessons we have learned from him. One of these lessons concerned time and the power of a minute. What can you do in a minute? You can change your whole life! The minute you say, "It's over, or let's begin, or I quit, or I will, or never again, or I do," your life changes. And every day, we get 1,440 minutes of opportunities to choose how to spend our time and how to change our lives.

I was confronted head on about the importance of time and priorities in August 2011 when my mom was diagnosed with pancreatic cancer. Thirty-two days later, she was gone. During that short time, barely a month, I was by her hospital bed, holding her hand, brushing her hair, rubbing lotion on her arms, and talking with her. When time is limited, every moment becomes more precious. My entire focus shifted to caring for my mom. Of course, I had other things to do, other places I could be, and other projects waiting. My to-do list was long. Nevertheless, I *chose* to be with my mom. I delegated or set aside everything else, and I was present with her. In the past, I struggled with being present. When I was in one place, I would be thinking of all of the other things I should be doing instead. However, during this time with my mom, I was where I needed to be. I am so grateful that I was with her, where I mattered most.

Six months after my mom passed away, my long-time boyfriend, Joel, was diagnosed with cancer. Once again, while I was still grieving the loss of my mom, life was again flipped on its head. It became a series of doctor's appointments, cancer education, organizing prescriptions, surgery, chemo, radiation, complications, hospitals stays, and a stem cell transplant. Life became extremely focused for me and very narrow. My once big life of traveling, adventures, exploring, and lots of work suddenly became very small. I was deliberate in choosing where I went and how I spent my time. Events, activities, and invitations that I enjoyed were set aside to focus on Joel's health and spending time with him. Both during my time with my mom and then with Joel, I heard the words within me clearly saying, "Be where it matters most."

Praise God, Joel's transplant and cancer treatment was a success, and a couple of years after his initial diagnosis, he was declared in remission. Soon after that, I saw Dave when he came to San Diego for a speaking engagement. Over several conversations we had during the following months, the idea of this book came to life. It was during one of these conversations that I was sharing with him the journey I had been on: the insights I had, how my priorities about how I spent my time had shifted, and how I had, by design, been living my life with the new motto, "Be where it matters most." From these conversations, the idea of *Moments Matter* was born.

From my darkest times, I want to shed some light: Life is short. Your choices create the life you live, so choose to be where it matters most. My hope is that this book inspires you and reminds you of the importance of the moments that matter.

–Cindy

"Sometimes you will never know the value of a moment until it becomes a memory."
–Dr. Seuss

"Live in the present,
launch yourself on every wave,
find eternity in each moment."
–Henry David Thoreau

ACKNOWLEDGMENTS

"If I have seen further,
it is by standing on the shoulders of giants."
–Bernard of Chartres

I could not have written this book without the values my mother and father instilled in me. They passed away way too early in life, but they were both instrumental in how they raised me, the discipline they installed in me, and the mindset that there is no "can't."

My wife Terri has always been there with me even though we may have been thousands of miles apart. Her love and support were there when I realized my mission. She gave me her "go for it" to pursue it when it would have been much easier to just live our lives instead of fulfilling my mission. To my children who have always been my best cheerleaders. I love all of you very much. I am grateful for your understanding in granting me the time I needed to pursue my mission and write this book.

Bishop Ken Carter was instrumental in helping me understand the real meaning of faith. He was the first to fully see, hear, know, and bring out my speaking ministry, which gave me the motivation to go pursue the "Great Commission."

There were unbelievable people who helped me on this journey. When I was getting inundated for requests, I needed people who not only appreciated what happened to me, but could handle the logistics behind the scenes and be a support structure to reinforce that I was on the right "flight pattern." Tammy, Lisa, Vickie, and Cindy, I want to thank you for being there. You all were there when times were great and when we faced challenges. You gave me inspiration and support and for that I'll never forget you.

When I started my time with the Anthony Robbins security team, I didn't really know what it entailed, but I followed the lead of the leaders of the team so I could be the best I could be. When I accepted the opportunity to serve as the leader of the team, Mike Melio was my "wingman." He became not only a strong friend, but gave me many life lessons when I needed strength. I want to thank him for being there with and for me and on January 15, 2009, was the one that thought enough about me to let our teammates know what happened.

I often speak about Tony Robbins. I first met Tony in 1994 on a break he was having in one of his events. He was kind to sign a picture for me, which I still have. When I volunteered for his event staff, he didn't know who I was, but I was honored to be there serving. At his event in Maui, I was asked to support his green room by making sure he could have the time and space to do his magic. One event later, I was asked to sit on stage left to watch his back. For the next 10 years, I watched his back in many different roles, ultimately becoming his director of security. He was always there giving me coaching and guidance. He always saw a "bigger me" than I ever thought and he brought that inner strength out of me which gave me the push to make the impact I am now able to make around the world. For that, I'll always be grateful. If I can impact $1/100000^{th}$ of the people he has, my mission will be realized.

The American Red Cross has a very special spot in my heart. Not only were they there at the pier in New Jersey and later that night in the hospital giving me much needed clothing, but most importantly, the next day they were with my family at Charlotte Douglass Airport. Pam Jeffers was supporting my family in time of confusion and for that I'll always be grateful. When Pam called and asked for my help, there was no second thinking. Her reaching out to me led me to be able to support the Red Cross around the country, and in 2016, around the world. I made a goal, and let the Red Cross leadership know, that my goal was to have the "Miracle" have impact in every state so others could be touched the way I was. They were not only there for me at a time when my life was in jeopardy, but there for and with me to help me support them as they support others who are in crisis. The Red Cross truly has a spiritual mission.

And finally I want to thank Cindy Wrightson for her leadership and assistance in reviewing the events and lessons in this book and supplementing my thoughts with her own. While her help has been invaluable throughout the writing process, I take responsibility for the content of this book. Any errors and/or omissions are mine alone.

Without all of you, I would not be who or where I am today. I am honored to be your friend and family, thank you from the bottom of my heart. – Dave

With heartfelt gratitude, I thank:

Dave – for trusting me with your words. It's an honor to be your friend and support you in spreading your mission.

Joel, Max, and Molly – you bring meaning to my life and a deeper appreciation for the moments we share. I love you!

Laurie Thompson – my best friend of 32 years. You're my life preserver, my soul sister, and cheerleader. My life is better because you're in it.

Pam Hendrickson – I'm grateful for the moment you decided to hire me to join the Creative department at RRI. That moment changed my life for the better and it's because of you. Your friendship, love, guidance, and support is priceless.

Tony Robbins – having the privilege to support you made me a stronger and better person. You've helped me realize what I am capable of and my life looks completely different because I met you. Thank you! – Cindy

INTRODUCTION

THE 12 RESOURCES TO CREATE YOUR PERSONAL FLIGHT PLAN

**"It is in your moments of decision
that your destiny is shaped."**
–Anthony Robbins

In 1985, I was fortunate to come across a person who took a great interest in me. His name was Bill, and he was in his 60s when I first met him. He was a highly successful businessman in Charlotte, North Carolina and one of the few people I had ever met who actually walked his talk. At a seminar in 1992, which was the first personal development seminar I had attended, Tom Hopkins suggested taking successful people out to lunch to find out their strategies, so I went to Bill and took him to lunch to ask him what it took for him to become a business leader. Bill gave me a life lesson. He told me that if I wanted anything in life, I needed to put myself in the proximity of the kind of people I wanted to be. It was a great lesson to have, especially at a young age.

I was excelling at ADP, the company I was with at the time, but I wanted an edge to take me from just receiving the monthly sales target plaque to being recognized as the best in the company. I was therefore driven to be the best I could be. I had a young family and wanted to give them everything I could in order to have the best opportunity to achieve

1

whatever they wanted. I took Bill's advice, and the following year, I was one of the top producers at ADP; I was at the pinnacle of what could be achieved there. However, I wanted more.

I had heard about another motivational speaker who was my age and living his dream—Tony Robbins. I asked myself, why him and not me? What was the difference? So, in 1994, I signed up for his seminar at San Diego, California, paying $4000 to attend (my wife thought I had fallen off the deep end). It was a small fortune, but I knew I was investing in my dream of becoming a business leader. I attended the seminar with about 350 other business leaders and those who wanted to be business leaders. It was amazing to experience such energy, focus, and commitment to be leaders. On day three of the seminar (at around 2:00 a.m., after an 18 hour stint the previous day), we were asked to write our personal mission statements. I didn't know what a mission statement was, but I had paid the money and was all in. With the song "Mysterious Ways" by U2 playing, I wrote my personal mission statement on October 4, 1994:

> *I, Dave Sanderson, see, hear, feel and know that the purpose of my life is to be happy. I realize that I can accomplish anything I desire when I have faith in my Creator and inspiring others to do the same.*

I put my pencil down and reread it, over and over. Tony told us the next day (which was, in fact, later the same day) that we needed to internalize it so that it became us. He was living his dream, and I was not, so I was going to follow his instruction. I internalized it and didn't look at it again for months as Tony had told us that we may be inclined to change it. After about six months, I went back to it and noticed that I wasn't living it. I was successful, had lost 20 pounds, was still a top producer at ADP, and had another child on the way, but I was not happy with myself. That is when you start realizing that God's delays are not God's denials, and I started to refocus instead on contributing my time to support others in search of their personal improvement. For the next 15 years, I volunteered to support Tony's work, to the point of ultimately becoming his security director in 2004. Whenever I had opportunities to speak with Tony, he asked me why I was working for a company and not for myself. Good question. I guess I had a fear of the unknown, whether it be money, insurance, recognition, whatever. In 2009, that all changed.

On January 15, 2009, I was a top-notch tech sales manager. I had finished work sooner than anticipated and wanted to get home. Luckily for me, my travel agent was able to procure a seat on an earlier flight from New York's LaGuardia Airport bound for Charlotte, North Carolina. A few moments after departure, a flock of Canada geese collided with US Airways Flight 1549, crippling both engines on its initial climb. Captain Chesley B. "Sully" Sullenberger knew that he couldn't make it to a nearby airport, and took the only option left: to attempt a successful water landing on the Hudson River. He was successful, and that incredible feat, which saved the lives of 155 passengers and crew, became known as the Miracle on the Hudson.

I was one of the last passengers off that plane. I didn't intend to be last, but as I headed toward the nearest exit, I heard my late mother's voice in my head, saying, "If you do the right thing, God will take care of you." So, I did what I thought was the right thing and stayed behind to help those who needed it to get off the plane first. When I was finally plucked from the frigid waters of the Hudson River and rushed to a nearby hospital, very little time had elapsed.

It took only 30 minutes for my life to change forever. Moments matter. All of a sudden, the mission that I had written down on October 4, 1994, was realized. I had faith in my Creator, and now, I had the opportunity to inspire others. I realized that life is more about how can I contribute to others than it being about my own personal significance. I was also reminded that nothing in life is certain. Those who are resourceful and can anticipate and focus on the wellbeing of others will grow into their ultimate purpose in life.

That was the genesis of what is known as my "halftime" experience and reinventing the second half of my life. This book is not only a look into the key resources that I and others used that day on the Hudson River, but it also teaches the importance of understanding, each day, that you have a mission on this earth. Your mission may not be apparent when you want it to be, but it will be revealed to you if you do the right things in life. By no means have I done everything right in my life (no one has, except the one Divine Being who walked the earth); nevertheless, what my mom told me was correct: "If you do the right thing, God will take care of you." On the Hudson, after hearing the words of my mother, I knew what the right thing was and did it.

I want to explain, in the simplest of terms, an extraordinary event that changed the life of one ordinary person forever, focusing on the key personal resources that this person and others drew upon that day. My hope is that, when you encounter your own "personal plane crash" in life, whether illness, a house fire, an automobile accident, or some other traumatic incident, you too can call on one or all of these key resources, not only to survive but also to thrive and live your life's mission.

In these pages, I share resources to ultimately live your mission and fulfillment in your life. I hope you find it a practical and valuable resource. I know that as this book goes out among people everywhere, it will change the lives of many, hopefully for the better.

"The Miracle on the Hudson was a reaffirmation that people really can be good at what they do, they can be heroic."

–Geraldo Rivera

JANUARY 15, 2009

What if you knew that you had only one minute left to live? Would all the moments in your life really matter? On January 15, 2009, another tragedy really could have happened in New York City. Instead, a miracle occurred. There were 155 people on US Airways Flight 1549, and I was just one of those that day who were blessed.

In the next several pages, I'm going to share with you that experience on Flight 1549 and some of the things I was thinking. There were specific resources used that I believe really contributed to it becoming known as "The Miracle on the Hudson." Whether it was due to teamwork, leadership, resourcefulness, knowing how to manage one's mind during a crisis, or the power of faith, certainty and courage created a miraculous outcome out of a very chaotic and potentially tragic situation.

30 Minutes for a Life to Change Forever

One thing I would like for you to think about as I tell you this story is this: from the time the plane took off from LaGuardia Airport to the time it crashed in the Hudson River to the time I got to the hospital was only about 30 minutes.

I wasn't scheduled to be on this flight. I was scheduled to be on the 5:00 p.m. flight. That day, I was working at a distribution center in Brooklyn, New York, where I was a sales manager. I don't know if you know anyone who has ever worked at a distribution center, but they normally open quite early. This one opened up at 2:00 a.m. I started my day at about 5:00 a.m. and finished at about 10:00 a.m.

I travel over 100,000 miles a year with my job, so I usually try to take advantage of any chance to get home to my wife and four kids a little early. At about 10:00 a.m., I called our travel agent, who booked me on Flight 1549. I truly believe that I was supposed to be on that plane for a reason.

There was nothing extraordinary about the day. It was 11 degrees and snowing. I was one of the first set of passengers to board the plane because of my top-tier status with US Airways. I went back to my seat, 15A, which was four rows behind the left wing. I did exactly what I did every single time I got on a plane then, and I'm guessing it's what you do when you get on a plane now. I went back to my seat, put my briefcase down, put my wallet in the briefcase, pulled a magazine out, and started to read. I did not listen to the flight crew, I did not know where the exits were, and I did not read that little brochure they always tell you to read. I guarantee you every single time I get on a plane now I do, because now I know how important it is to be aware when on an airplane.

A little over 60 seconds after we took off is when I heard an explosion. I wasn't aware that we were hit by a bird strike – a collision between our aircraft and a flock of Canadian Geese

– which disabled both engines. It was a loud explosion, and I'd never heard any sound like this on a plane before, so it got my attention. I looked out the window and saw fire coming out from beneath the left wing. I knew something had happened, but I fly so often that I thought our plane had just lost an engine. No big deal. It really didn't startle me too much. That's where I think God's grace entered for the first moment on this flight, because no one on that plane knew at that moment in time that what had happened on the left side had also happened on the right side of the plane.

I truly believe that if anybody were to have cross-referenced or checked in and started asking, "What did you see? What did you hear?" there could have been a lot of panic. We didn't know both engines were gone. When people panic, people lose their heads, and when people lose their heads, they start making irrational decisions. To this day, the one thing that stays with me is that it was so quiet you could hear a pin drop. The guy sitting next to me elbowed me and asked, "Hey, man, what's going on?" I said, "I think he's going back to LaGuardia." I felt the plane turning, and I thought we were just going back to the airport.

Fortunately for all of us, we had a captain who not only had 40 years of experience and 20,000 hours of flight time but had also been a fighter jet pilot during the Vietnam War. As important, if not more important, is that our first officer, Jeff Skiles, also had over 20,000 hours of flight experience. The captain, Chesley "Sully" Sullenberger, was also a certified glider expert, and he had to employ that skill of gliding to save me, 154 other souls, and possibly the George Washington Bridge in New York.

As soon as he cleared the bridge, he said the only words he said throughout the entire time on the plane: "This is your captain. Brace for impact."

As I mentioned, I hadn't paid attention to the preflight instructions, so I didn't know what that meant, but I knew it was serious. Let me give you a heads-up: if you ever hear that on a plane, something's going down, and it's going down fast.

I think that was the moment that everything I learned and everything I trained for came together. For the 10 years prior to that day, I had been the head of security for Tony Robbins. If you've never heard of Tony Robbins, he's an inspiring speaker, entrepreneur, author, and peak-performance strategist. I highly recommend that you check him out. As the head of security, I not only had the opportunity to travel with Tony but was also able to learn and absorb everything that he taught, in addition to having access to all the incredible people with whom he spent time.

As soon as the captain cleared the George Washington Bridge, I did two things. The first thing I did was pray. I prayed for whoever the captain was. I prayed that he would just get me down in one piece. I didn't want to end up in multiple body parts; I wanted to at least remain one unit. The second thing I prayed for was that the last person I spoke with, who was my client in Brooklyn, would call my wife and tell her I love her. The third prayer was to God to forgive my sins. I didn't want anything between Him and me at this point. We were going down, and I wanted to go up, and it was not looking good for me right now. The second thing I did was reach down in my briefcase and grab my wallet. I shoved it down into my pants, because if something did happen—and it looked as if it was probably going to happen—at least they would be able to claim my body. Then, I put my head down.

It was between 60 and 70 seconds after we cleared the bridge that we crashed into the river, and it was a hard hit. Captain Sullenberger estimates that we were going between 100 and 120 miles per hour. That's how hard a hit it was. I was pushed all the way back and up in my seat. It was that hard of a hit. When I came back up, I opened my eyes, and I looked out the window. I saw light coming through the window, so I knew I had a shot, but I wasn't out of trouble.

It could have been a bigger tragedy than anybody could ever imagine, but Captain Sullenberger hit the water perfectly. However, getting us down safely was only half of it. Once we were down, we had to get out because the plane was sinking into the Hudson River.

When the plane landed, the entire bottom was stripped off. Someone had actually listened to the flight crew when they'd said "The closest exit may be behind you," and he tried to open the door at the back of the plane. Immediately, water was coming in from underneath the plane, as well as from the back of the plane.

Getting Everyone Out

Depending on where you were on that plane—and I was toward the back—water was immediately ankle to knee to waist deep . . . just like that. The question I get asked all the time during the Q&A portion of the presentations I give is "How did the people get on the wings so fast?" The image people remember from this whole day is of people standing on the wings of an airplane in the middle of a river. As I mentioned when we hit, I was pushed back in my seat, and the top of the seat broke. When the top of the seats broke, people became extremely resourceful. All of a sudden, people started jumping on top of the seats and walking down the seats to get out to the exit. That's how most people got out. I didn't do that; I didn't think about getting on top of the seat. When it was my time to go, my game plan was "Get to the aisle, get up, and get out." It was exactly my first thought: "Get up the aisle, and get out of the plane."

When I got to the aisle, something happened that not only changed that day for me, but it also probably changed the entire direction of where I was going to go. I heard my mother speak to me. My mom had passed away in 1997. There was something she would tell me as a child that just popped in my head in that moment: "If you do the right thing, God will take care of you." So I had to make a choice. What was the right thing to do? I grew up playing sports, and I had been a Boy Scout; we were taught to do the right thing. At that moment in time, the right thing for me was to take care of other people first. That's how I became the last passenger off the plane. I wasn't injured, and I thought I could take care of myself.

Once everybody was out, it was my turn to go. But not only had the tops of the seats broken back, but the bins had broken open, too. Now, there was luggage falling out, I was waist-deep in water, it was dark at the back of the plane, it was late afternoon in winter, and there weren't any lights working on the plane. So, every time I took a step, I hit something. At that point, I couldn't see what I was hitting. Was it somebody's body? Was it luggage? So, every step was made with purpose. It was like, What did I hit? What did I hit now? The furthest I could get up to was seat 10F on the right side of the plane.

The first picture that was released on Good Morning America was of me trying to get out of the plane. When I reached the exit, it was an amazing sight. There was no room on the wing for me, there was no room on the boat for me, but it was an amazing sight. People were already being rescued. I don't know who said this on TV—and I heard it a couple times—but whoever said it got it right. He said, "Sullenberger and Skiles got the plane down, and the crew and passengers got the people out, but the real heroes of the day were the first responders." The first of the first responders was the New York Waterways, the ferries. They were there about two minutes after the plane crashed. There are numerous ways to define what a miracle is, and to have someone there to rescue you just a couple minutes after a plane crash, in ice cold water, is a miracle.

At this point, I was standing waist-deep in the 36-degree water, leaning out of the exit door, and holding onto this little inflatable lifeboat. The Hudson River has an extremely fast current. The plane actually floated about half a mile down the river in 24 minutes, so the little lifeboat kept floating away from the plane. And like me, no one in the lifeboat read the instructions. No one knew that it was actually tethered to the plane. So, as they were floating further out into the river and away from the plane, they kept screaming to me, "Hold on! Hold on!" I was the only person left on that side of the plane who had leverage. So I held onto the plane and held onto the boat as closely as I could so they wouldn't float away.

Then, all of sudden, I turned and saw something that caught my eye. It was a lady standing on the wing, and she was holding a baby. I found out later that she had two kids on the plane. She had a three-year-old on that lifeboat and the three-month-old she was holding. She wasn't moving. I'm sure she was scared. Not only was it 36-degree water, but there was also jet fuel all over the place, and it was slick. There were people sliding all over the place. So the lady with the baby was standing in the middle of the wing, and she wasn't moving.

In that moment, all the things I've learned in my life, all the teams I've been on with corporations, and all my training said, "If you've got somebody in that trance situation, where they can't do anything, you have to do something radical to break them out of it." So, I yelled at her: "Throw the baby! Throw the baby!" I knew she wasn't going to throw her baby. I didn't think that was an option she was going to employ, but I did get her attention. When I yelled at her, it startled her enough, and I broke her trance.

It's amazing where God puts people in times of crisis. All of a sudden, this mother of three from Knoxville, Tennessee heard me yell this at this lady. She then looked at her and said, "Give me the baby. Give me the baby." The lady turned and gave her the baby, jumped on the lifeboat, and all 60 people on the wing were able to get off the plane.

Awhile after the crash, the lady with the baby sent me a package. It had two things in it. The first was a note that said, "Thank you for saving my family." The second was a picture of Captain Sullenberger with the baby from that day as a thank-you and a reminder of what we all did that day together as a team.

Once she got in the lifeboat and people began walking down the wing to be rescued, that's when I started thinking of my strategy to get out. At this point, I was still on the plane. I had been up to my waist in ice-cold 36-degree water for seven minutes.

Then, one of the boats hit the front of the plane. That's not that big of a deal, unless you're on the plane, which I was. Once that happened, I felt the cold water start to slosh and go up my back. I feared the plane was going down like the boat did in Titanic when it tipped and sucked everything down in the water. I thought, I do not want to be sucked down with this plane. That's when I made the decision that it was time for me to get off the plane. I swam to the closest ferry that I could find, which was at the end of the wing. That's how I got off the plane. I thank my parents for forcing me to take swimming lessons when I was a kid, because if it weren't for them, I may never have been able to get off that plane.

Getting off the Plane

Once I got onto the ferry, we went to the New Jersey side of the river. I found out later that this was because of the way the plane was positioned. Whatever closest point to shore you were is where you were going to go. The left side was facing Manhattan, and the right side was facing Hoboken, New Jersey. Since I was on the right side of the plane, I ended up in New Jersey. I found out later that they had radioed ahead because they knew I had been in the water for several minutes. When we hit the shore, there were three people waiting for me. There were two EMTs and a gentleman from the American Red Cross who was waiting with a blanket. That's why I speak all over the country now for the American Red Cross.

A little-known fact about that day is that there were a lot of groups who helped out, but there were two groups that touched everyone: The ferries and the Red Cross on both the New York and New Jersey side.

Once I got to the shore, I couldn't walk. They had to pick me up and carry me to the triage center. I don't know if you know what a triage center is, but it's a room with nothing in it. There's nothing special about a triage center. They put me next to the wall, stripped off all my clothes down to my skivvies, and all of a sudden, Heather, my EMT, said, "I'll be right back."

At this point, I was on the floor in my underwear. I didn't even know where I was. I looked to one side, and there was a guy sort of like me. I looked to the other side, and there was a girl who didn't even have underwear on.

It's amazing; when you're naked on the floor and no one's talking. All I could think was, "What's going on now? I'm naked on the floor with two people I don't even know." All of a sudden I looked up, and there was a guy walking toward me. He had a card in his hand, and he came up to me and said, "Sir, I need your name, and I need your date of birth." I got the words out, and he wrote it on the card, taped it to my right ankle, and just walked away. I don't know if you remember the TV show from the 1970s called *M*A*S*H* about a team of army doctors during the Korean War. If they tag your toe, they're carting you out. Game over, you didn't make it. That's exactly what I thought. It's like the movie *Ghost*, with Patrick Swayze: you watch yourself die, you have no control, you're talking, and no one's answering. It's true, I thought. I'm dying, I'm dying. I didn't make it.

Then Heather came back and said, "I'm going to take your blood pressure." She put on the cuff. Good, I thought, I have blood pressure; that's a good thing to have. Unfortunately, it was 190/120, and she looked at me and said, "You've got to go STAT." I'd heard that one on TV before. If something's going to happen, they say, "STAT." She said, "We've got to go STAT. You can have a heart attack or stroke. We've got to go right now." My first thought was, I survived a plane crash. I got out of the water, and now I'm going to die of a heart attack or stroke. It just keeps coming. Now we were in fast motion. They put me on a gurney and started wheeling me out.

Getting to the Hospital

The place where we were had glass doors in the back, so, suddenly, I was looking out wondering, What's going on? They opened the doors, and there was media everywhere. I have never seen media like this in my life. The medical personnel were trying to get me to the ambulance, and a guy from NBC had his camera and a story: "Last Passenger Out." He started following us. They were trying to get me in the ambulance, he was jumping into the ambulance, and there was chaos in the ambulance. They got security, got everything cleaned up, closed the doors, and took me to the hospital. We arrived at the Palisades Medical Center a few miles away, and there were 20 or 30 people waiting just for me.

Ten women with blankets picked me up because I had severe hypothermia and couldn't use my legs, and they couldn't get the gurney out of the ambulance. It was locked in there. They carried me to a hospital bed, where there was a doctor waiting. Now it was go time. The doctor started yelling out orders. He said, "Blood pressure?" They took it again: 190/120. I knew it wasn't good. The tech said I could die of a heart attack or stroke. That was not good. He said, "Oxygen?" They yelled out, "75!" I didn't know what that meant, but I found out later that this was not good either. Then, he said, "Temperature?" They took it orally and it was 96. He yelled out "Anally!" I got that one, right? It was going down; whether I liked it or not, it was coming my way. Nurse Bautista was my angel; she stayed with me the entire night. She screamed at the doctor, "I can't get them off! I can't get them off!" What happened was that my body was so cold and wet that my underwear was sticking and frozen to my hips. I still have scars on my hips from them trying to get them off. What do nurses always have? Scissors that are like a foot long, right? She reached down and went clip, clip, rip. That fast, and it was done; my underwear was off. All I had left was my watch. My temperature was 94 degrees, and they diagnosed me with hypothermia. My body was so cold that it took them five hours to warm me up and basically get me back to room temperature.

That was an amazing five hours. During that time, I met the former governor of New Jersey, as well as the heads of the Port Authority, the FBI, Homeland Security, the New York State Police, and the New Jersey State Police. They all wanted to talk to me and another gentleman from the plane, Barry Leonard, who was there with me. He was the first passenger out and had been in seat 1C. When they'd said to evacuate, he'd jumped into the water, fallen flat on the water, and fractured his sternum. The reason they wanted to talk to us is that we were accessible. Out of 150 passengers, only two people stayed overnight in the hospital—Barry and me.

Out of 150 people, 148 went home that night just a few hours after a plane crash in the ice-cold water. That's why the governor of New York named the event a miracle; that's how it got the name. I even remember that night as I watched the footage from my hospital bed. Details of the crash weren't released for a couple of hours because the authorities couldn't account for everybody; everybody had started going home.

The authorities knew where we were, and they had questions. One of the questions I got was, "Do you think this was a terrorist attack?" If you have a plane going toward a bridge and toward Manhattan, somebody has to answer questions. That night, the crew from the flight was locked down in their hotel for the whole night. You didn't see the crew. Everyone else had gone home, so we were answering those kinds of questions all night long.

In addition, I kept telling the doctor, "I have no clothes. I have no clothes." The doctor said, "Why do you need clothes? You're in a hospital." I'd never overnighted in a hospital, so I didn't know you didn't need any clothes. What the doctor didn't know was this: not only did all the authorities know where we were, but all the media also knew where we were. Barry and I were going to be on Good Morning America, The Early Show, and Fox and Friends, and I had nothing to wear. I had my watch; that's all I had.

Somebody from the Northern New Jersey Chapter of the American Red Cross went and got some really ugly sweats for me to wear the next day. You can go to my website and see the interview with me in the sweats. That totally stumped me: that somebody who didn't know me went out in the middle of the night and got me something to wear.

When something like this happens, US Airways and American have emergency response teams that they deploy. Each one of us was assigned our own team member. Mine was Doreen from Pittsburgh. She flew in the middle of the night, and she had one job: to take care of me.

With the media rush, my medical team trying to get me back to health, and everything else that was happening, I wasn't able to call my family. When Doreen showed up, she had a phone. She had me call my family, and I was able to speak with them for the first time at around midnight. At that point, I heard her story about what was going on at home, which was probably as exciting as what I was going through, because she had to deal with a lot of media at home.

Going Home to Charlotte

The next morning, Barry and I did the interviews. When I was done, I was feeling pretty good. I wanted to go home. Doreen said, "Listen, I don't want to put any more stress on you, but I'm going to put you on the 12:00pm flight home." I said, "I want to go home now." She said, "No, you don't understand. I can't get you to the airport now." I said, "No, you don't understand. My wife's at the airport in Charlotte with the kids. She's probably freaking out, and I want to go home now." She said, "You don't understand. You are in

20

Weehawken, New Jersey. You're going out of LaGuardia Airport in New York. It's 9:00 a.m. The flight leaves at 10:00 a.m. I can't get there in time."

I shared with you that the night before everyone had wanted to talk to me. Everyone had wanted to be my friend. They'd all left their business cards and said, "Call me if you need anything." So, I cashed in.

I'm going to tell you right now who the most important person in New York City is—the director of the Port Authority. I gave his business card to Doreen and said, "Call him. He said he'd help me." She looked at me with big eyes, "Call the director of the Port Authority?" I repeated, "Call him! He said he'd help me." She later told me, "I thought you were freaking out; I thought you were having a meltdown." She went outside and called the director of the Port Authority.

Six minutes later, I had a police escort. They took me from Weehawken, New Jersey to LaGuardia Airport in 16 minutes in a pimped-out Escalade, and I was in my hoodie. That's a miracle, right? If you ever have a chance to go through Manhattan in a police escort, take it. A few months ago, I did the same route, and it took me two and a half hours. It's amazing. So they were prepping me the whole way. I agreed to do one interview, but then I wanted to go home. I just wanted to get out of there. I didn't have any bags to check; my luggage was still in the Hudson River. I was ready to go. We all forgot one major detail though: I didn't have any identification. Everybody forgot, including me.

How am I going to get through security without ID? I gave

the Homeland Security guy's business card to the TSA agent. The TSA agent looked at me as if to say, "Why would I call the director of New Jersey Homeland Security?" I said, "He knows who I am. Please call him." He did, and I was able to get through a New York airport's security without ID. That's a miracle. Try that with TSA; it doesn't work.

I got through security and now had a big entourage. They were all walking down to the gate with me. We got to the gate, and there was some commotion going on. They accompanied me right onto the plane. What I found out later is that the captain deboarded the plane when he found out that I was going to be on his flight. He had been ready to go, but he deboarded the airplane because he and the first officer wanted to interview me.

They had never talked to anybody who'd survived a plane crash. Who talks to anybody who survives a plane crash? They never had. He said he wanted to have a one-on-one interview with me. We sat down in first class, and we talked. He had questions, but what he wasn't expecting was that I also had questions for him. "Are you going to get me over the bridge? Are you going to get me home?" He looked at me and said, "Sir, I don't have gliding experience." That was the first time I had ever heard that. All these pilots don't have the same experience. He said, "But I will get you home safe. What I'll do for you is this: when we hit 3,300 feet . . ." That was the first time I'd heard that information. I didn't know how high the plane had ever gotten. He continued, "I will ring the bell so you and I will know where this happened yesterday."

I flew back in coach. I didn't get first class, but I did get free potato chips and soda. Their flight attendant, Beth, took great care of me. She put me in the middle seat with no one beside me so I'd have extra space. I put my hoodie on. I looked like the Unabomber, and I crouched forward and braced myself for the flight. I didn't want to talk to anybody. Then, I heard ding, ding, ding. I looked out the window and was surprised because I realized that 3,300 feet is not that high up.

Suddenly, it started coming back to me. That was the moment when I started to realize what really happened. Not only was it unbelievable what Captain Sullenberger did but also what Jeff Skiles did as the first officer. He and I spoke at a Red Cross event a few years ago in Chattanooga, Tennessee. He shared the perspective from the front of the plane, and I talked about what happened at the back of the plane. It was a very cool talk. It was two hours, and we got to tell the whole story. I learned some things. One thing I learned from Jeff was that the first officer has a book in the cockpit called How Do You Get Down from an Emergency from 30,000 Feet? He did it from 3,000 feet. He was telling Captain Sullenberger step by step what to do. He's as much of a hero as Captain Sullenberger, but you rarely hear about the second guy in command.

Now, we were on our final descent on the flight back to Charlotte. I hadn't spoken to anyone but the flight attendant. The guy two seats over from me opened up to page four of Newsday. What's on page four of Newsday? A photo of me in the hospital. He looked at me and asked, "Are you that guy on the plane?" I asked, "What?" And he turned to show me my picture. I was thinking, Man, my picture's in the paper.

He said, "You were that guy on that plane." He said it out

loudly so that everybody heard it. Now everybody got out of their seats wondering, Who is this guy? Then, the flight attendants were saying, "Get down. Get in your seats. Get down." Beth came running down the aisle and asked, "Are you okay?" I said, "Yeah, just take me off this plane last." That was the first thing I felt: "Get me out of here, I'm not ready for this." When we landed, Beth was like my guardian angel. She stepped right up, and no one got to me; she took care of it. She escorted me off the plane last, and my family was there, US Airways was there to greet me, and the CEO of the American Red Cross was there with my family. By far, that was the most important thing that happened that entire day.

A Mission Realized

In the years since the plane crash, I've had the honor of going to places such as Fort Hood after the shootings, Oklahoma after the tornadoes, and a few years ago, to the eastern shore of North Carolina after Super Storm Sandy. I've had the chance to talk with people who go through crisis. One of the things I found out over all these times that I've been able to go to places for the Red Cross is that people like me get taken care of. I'm out front, so I get taken care of. It's often the families who are forgotten, and the Red Cross was there taking care of my family. That's why I speak so passionately for the Red Cross. That's where my miracle turned into my mission.

The Sunday after the plane crash my mission was realized. I went to my church, and everybody wanted to talk to me, but there was one guy who really wanted to talk to me. He was the head of the men's breakfast. He came walking up to me and said, "Dave, will you speak next Sunday at our breakfast?" I said, "No, problem." I thought, Fifty guys eating pancakes; that's a walk in the park. No problem. I didn't know that they had advertised all over Charlotte and that 500 to 600 people would show up. They had to move it into the gym to fit everyone. And it was daunting.

So, I was in a gym with a stage at one end with a curtain. I went behind the curtain and prayed, "God give me something to say and give it to me now. Deliver it." I got up in front of everyone, I said whatever I said that day, and I finished speaking. Two gentlemen wanted to talk to me. One was from Wachovia Bank. They had people who were on the plane with me. We were talking for a few minutes. All of a sudden, I looked up toward the back of the room and saw this lady lock eyes with me. She was 80 or 90 years old at least. She started making her way up to me. She interrupted this conversation and grabbed my arm very tightly. I jumped. A week after a plane crash, I was still a little dicey. My body was also bruised and hadn't healed yet, so when she touched me, it hurt. Then, she looked me in the eye and said, "I was questioning if there really is a God, and I don't believe in miracles. But you . . . you are physical evidence that there is a God and He performs miracles. Thank you, thank you." She let my arm go, looked me in the eye one more time, and just walked away. I've never seen her again. I then turned back to these two gentlemen, and I'd never seen two men cry like this—physically crying.

My minister was in the back watching all this, and I was looking at him wondering, What's going on? All of a sudden, it hit me. What happened to me on January 15, 2009 had an impact on somebody. And that's what set me on my journey.

Think back to 2009. There weren't many positive things happening in this country. Financially, things weren't good; whether it was real estate or banking, things were pretty negative. Then, all of sudden, a captain and a crew and passengers did something that had never ever been done in the history of aviation. One team, one goal, one miracle. It gave people hope.

There's a passage in the Bible that says, "Suffering produces endurance, endurance produces character, character produces hope, and hope does not disappoint us." That's not only what happened that day, but that's also what I have the honor of doing every single day all over the world. Success leaves clues, which is why I'm driven to share what I've learned, because I never know who I might impact.

Mission-Focused Leadership

One of the things I do when I speak to corporations is I talk about teamwork, leadership, and some of the resources that we used that day. For example, back in 1999, I had the honor and privilege of escorting General Norman Schwarzkopf. He was a four-star general for the United States Army. I had 45 minutes with him. I don't know if you've ever been around a four-star general, but it can be pretty intimidating.

I asked him, "General, do you mind if I ask you a question?" He looked at me and said, "No one ever asks a general a second question." I thought, Oh, I made the general mad already. He looked at me and said, "Go ahead, ask your question." I said, "Thank you. I have one question. How did you win that war in Iraq so quickly?" He responded, "Are you just asking, or do you really want to know?" I said, "I really want to know, sir." He told me he had to get everybody aligned with the mission.

He looked at me and said, "Every day, I had people coming to me with problems, such as women can't drive in Saudi Arabia, or women have to cover their faces, or they have to pray five times a day. I kept reminding them, how does that contribute to the mission of kicking Saddam out of Kuwait?" He told me that once he got people focused on the mission, everything started rolling.

He had one specific mission, which he focused everybody on and executed in record time. It taught me a great lesson about leadership. Leadership is stepping up, giving a mission to somebody, and helping them accomplish that mission. That's what happened on the plane that day.

Now, I have the opportunity to speak and share the lessons and strategies from that day with audiences all around the world. My desire and goal is that you might learn one or two things so that the next time you face what I call your own "personal plane crash"—whether that's cancer, a fire, a car accident, or whatever it may be—you, too, might be able to remember a couple of insights that I share that you can call on so you not only survive but also then thrive afterward.

"Other than hitting the birds,
everything went our way that day."
—First Officer Jeff Skiles

THE 12 RESOURCES

TO CREATE YOUR

PERSONAL FLIGHT PLAN

"A resourceful person can see opportunity when others only see obstacles."

–Garrett Gunderson

|1| AWARENESS

> "Everything happens for a reason
> and it has a purpose, and it serves me."
> –Anthony Robbins

Have you ever had something happen in your life that you didn't plan, never expected, and perhaps never would have wanted, but that completely changed your life for the better?

For me, that was Flight 1549.

On January 15, 2009, nothing about the flight was out of the ordinary. It was just another typical flight—until two minutes after takeoff, when the plane collided with a flock of Canadian geese that took out both engines, and I heard an explosion.

That was the first moment I became aware that something was wrong. Until that moment, I hadn't been paying attention to much of anything. Flying had become so routine for me that I did the same thing on almost every flight. The day I was a passenger on Flight 1549 was no different.

Something's very wrong

I was doing exactly what I did almost every flight: I had my head in a magazine. I wasn't paying attention to anything, including the pre-flight announcements. I wasn't aware that the geese were around, but when I heard the explosion, it definitely got my attention because that's one of those noises that you don't want to hear on a plane. So, I looked up from

31

my magazine and out the window, and I saw fire coming out from beneath the wing. I knew that something very serious had happened.

Once I was aware of something going on in the plane, my other resources started to kick it. Becoming aware allowed me to appropriately access these other resources of focus, faith, state management, teamwork, and sensory acuity.

I believe that one of the key reasons we achieved the outcome we did on the "Miracle on the Hudson" was the keen awareness of not only Captain Sullenberger, but also the crew and passengers. Luke 21:36 calls for us to "Stay awake at all times." That day, Captain Sullenberger had his flight plan, and First Officer Skiles was at the controls, but when the birds struck, Captain Sullenberger immediately took command of the plane. He was aware that First Officer Skiles had just been though simulator training on the complete emergency checklist—and, therefore, would be better able to know exactly which checklist to use and what to do in a short period of time. He was also acutely aware of his altitude, his airspeed, and the locations of nearby airports, all of which helped him assess his options.

When it was time to inform us—the passengers—of the situation, Captain Sullenberger was careful in what he said, "This is your captain. Brace for impact." He made sure that everyone was aware of the situation, but he also avoided inciting panic or putting the passengers and crew in a crisis mindset. That moment is when I became aware of the situation and forced myself into a high-awareness state.

One skill that I have learned and practiced is the skill of

sensory acuity. If I was going to have a chance of surviving the plane crash, I had to hone in on all my senses. I had to achieve optimal awareness.

I developed my flight plan in the 60+ seconds I and all the other passengers had after Captain Sullenberger made his famous statement: "Brace for impact." If the Captain could get the plane down and I was still alive, I had to execute.

When Captain Sullenberger landed the plane in the river, my sensory acuity kicked in. I was aware of what was going on around me, how others were reacting or not reacting, alternate pathways out of the plane, and who needed help. I could hear my mother speaking to me. It's amazing when you have a flight plan: Your awareness goes up to another level, and you can achieve things you never thought you could achieve.

Creating Raving Fans

There is another example of how awareness played into that day. I have to praise US Airways for how they handled my care during and after the plane crash. First, I was assigned a person from their emergency response team. She arrived soon after I got to the hospital and spent the evening and night with me. She was there to make sure that I was supported, not only immediately after the crash, but for a period of time afterward. In this way and others, US Airways was aware of its passengers' needs. We were provided an 800 number, a personal liaison for several weeks, and various other resources, including mental health support and compensation for lost belongings.

The awareness that US Airways showed and what the company did, both knowingly and unknowingly, were what turned me into raving fan. I now fly 95% of my flights on US Airways (which is now American), and I will be a diehard supporter for the rest of my life. By contrast, the company I worked for could have made me a raving fan by being aware of what I needed and providing a little space, time off, and support. But it didn't. Four and a half years after the plane crash, I left that organization because I didn't feel like I was supported.

Awareness comes in a lot of different ways. That day on the plane, one of the key reasons the situation turned out the way it did was that, once they realized that they were in a critical situation, so many of the passengers were not only aware of themselves, but also actively taking care of everybody else. That is what created the miracle.

Create Your Own Flight Plan
Tips to Improve Your Awareness

- Observe. Pay attention to what is going on around you
- Slow down and listen
- Use all of your senses
- Practice meditation
- Journal

"The event was a bookend.
The decade seemed to begin with people using airplanes as weapons and terrorism and ended with people coming together and saving a lot of lives."
–Chesley B. "Sully" Sullenberger, III

Next Steps
Let's stay connected! For more behind-the-scenes content, bonuses, videos, and updates, register this book at: www.momentsmatterbook.com

"Faith is the only thing I know of

that is stronger than fear."

–Joyce Meyer

|2| FAITH

"Suffering produces endurance,
endurance produces character,
character produces hope."
–Romans 5:3-4

The end of 2008 was rather bleak in the United States. Companies were filing for bankruptcy, the housing bubble had burst, and the financial sector had just discovered massive Wall Street fraud. But as the new year began, hope was restored when instead of catastrophe, a miracle happened on the Hudson River.

When Captain Sullenberger said, "This is your captain. Brace for impact," I looked around. Some people were locking arms, others were in prayer. I heard some people saying the Lord's Prayer. I braced my hands in front of me and started to pray. I prayed for the captain to get us down safely. I prayed for the strength to do the right thing. I prayed for forgiveness for my sins. I prayed for the safety of my wife and kids. I prayed that the last guy I talked to would call my wife and kids. Seconds later, we hit the water.

Trust and Faith

One of the lessons I learned from that day is that trust comes with conditions, but faith is unconditional. And in order to achieve the outcome that we did that day, we had to have faith in each other.

Later at the hospital, a chaplain came to see me. It was the first time I broke down. We prayed together and had a really long talk. He gave me a copy of the *New Testament*, just in case I needed it, and went out to the lobby to call my wife to tell her I was okay.

God's Hand Was on All of Us

I wasn't scheduled to be on Flight 1549. When I boarded the plane earlier that day, I had no way of knowing how profoundly my life was about to change. It was just a typical flight, until it wasn't. I think God put me there because it was my time to grow. He gave me the courage I needed to help others get off the plane and the strength to swim to the ferry. God's hand was on all of us. I believe He was showing us that there is hope.

Where a lot of my strength came from that day, and continues to come from, is my belief in God. You've got to believe in something bigger than yourself, whatever you may call it. Something that will be there for you, a rock that will be there for you, when things do get tough. In life, things will get tough. It's going to happen whether you like it or not. You don't have much control over what it will be, when it will happen, and what type of curveball you're going to get. Ultimately, what it comes down to is how you respond to each curveball and that you have faith that it's going to work out.

I'm often asked, "How has your faith changed since Flight 1549?" What happened to me that day was a strong testimonial for my faith. I always believed that there was a God, but it's imperative to have faith when things get tough.

I think what happened was a reminder for a lot of people that God is still around, God controls things, and He needed to show people that He *is* still around.

The weekend after the plane crash, there was a drawing in *The Sacramento Bee* called "God's Hands." It showed God's hands basically holding the plane up until everybody was safely off. It was an amazing way to depict what happened that day.

After Chesley "Sully" Sullenberger landed US Airways Flight 1549 in the Hudson River, *Sacramento Bee* editorial cartoonist Rex Babin imagined the passengers standing on the wings with the hands of God reaching down to keep the jet from sinking.

Create Your Own Flight Plan
Exercise

- What does having faith mean to you?

- What is your definition of faith?

- Is your faith consistent or does it change based on your circumstances? Why—or why not?

"The purpose is the why.
The destiny is the where."
–Bishop TD Jakes

Next Steps

Let's stay connected! Sign up to get my newsletter at http://davesandersonspeaks.com

|3| CERTAINTY

"Even though this was an unanticipated event for
which we have never specifically trained,
I was confident that I could quickly synthesize a
lifetime of training and experience, adapt it in a
new way to solve a problem I had never seen
before and get it right the first time, and so that's
what I did. In 208 seconds. I wasn't sure at the
outset exactly what steps I would take, but we
didn't have a lot of ambiguity: I knew what
happened. I didn't have to waste time with the
'what happened?' phase. I was able to go right to
the 'how do I fix this?' phase."
– Chesley B. "Sully" Sullenberger, III

One of the key reasons why people are successful in life is because they have certainty in the most uncertain of times. There's no more uncertain time as when you are going down in a plane crash, like I did on Flight 1549. I think that skillset, the ability to remain certain of your outcome even in a crisis, helped everybody on the plane that day. It not only helped me to be able to understand and make the decisions that I made on the plane, but it also helped me maintain control of myself and help the other passengers maintain control of their mindsets.

Finding Certainty in a Crisis

On the plane that day, certainty showed up in a lot of different ways. I think one of the things you realize when you're on a plane and something occurs is that you have no control. The only thing you can control is your mind. So, your certainty comes from your thought process. Fortunately for me on that day, I think all my certainty started coming from my thought process and how I was raised. I started thinking about things in the past, and in the last moments before the plane was going down into the river, I was thinking about everything in my life. All of a sudden, I was gaining certainty, so when we hit, whether I was going out of the plane alive or someplace else, I had certainty that *something* was going to happen.

So certainty was really driven from my thought process. I believe the perspective I got on certainty really started with my mom and my dad. My mother always told me, "You can do whatever you want if you believe in yourself." She always had certainty in each one of her children. I think it started there. I truly believe all the training that I've had in my life, and I think certainty comes from references in our lives. The more certainty you have, the more success you have. All of a sudden you get more certainty, so when that tough time comes you have something of a reference to draw upon.

For Captain Sullenberger, he went through Vietnam as a fighter jet pilot. He had 20,000 hours of flight time and 40 years of experience, so he had a lot of experience to draw on to give him certainty. So when that moment happened for him, he could draw upon that reference.

I was thinking in the last moments before the plane crashed, number one, I hope my wife does what I told her to do with the money (pay off the house and cover our kids' college tuition). Number two, I really was thinking I've done everything that I can. I have a pathway in life. Obviously, my pathway is going to take a different direction in the next coming moments, so prepare yourself for that. I did a final prayer. That was really the last thing that I did. I know I have another pathway, whether I'm going someplace else or coming back, it's going to happen here momentarily.

The Certainty Mindset

I was a sales person for 30 years. I still am. One of the things you learn in sales is that sales is really nothing more than helping people change their state of mind, to be able to believe in something that you believe is good for them. It's giving them certainty in your product and certainty in yourself. So, in business when tough times happen, you have to draw upon yourself and all the experiences you and your company have had.

In business, I drew certainty not only from my own knowledge and training, but also from my team. I had to have certainty in them that they were going to do and perform in the way they were supposed to in order to achieve the expected outcome.

I was in technology sales for 20 years. Technology sales is up and down. It's an industry that when it's hot, it's hot and when it's not, it's not – no one's going to spend a million dollars for a piece of software. How can you still perform in those kinds of uncertain times? Leaders step up at the most uncertain times. People will go to the person with the most certainty during the most uncertain times. When you're a leader of a team, like I was in sales and I am now at my own company, everybody looks to you for certainty. If you're uncertain, they're going to be uncertain. You set the tone.

The way you get certain is how you focus your mind. It's putting yourself in the proper state. I talk about state management all the time when I speak to audiences, and I believe the one thing you can do is control your mind and what you focus on. In addition, see things as they are, not worse than they are. Be honest in your assessment of the situation. Every time you want to get in a positive certain state, you look for references. I look for references. That's how I do it.

Certainty on Flight 1549

Certainty showed up on the plane that day as leaders stepped up. You could tell the people on that plane who had either some leadership background or had that innate ability to lead. Yes, Captain Sullenberger, of course, being the captain, was a leader and gave directions. There were several other leaders on the plane. That's one thing I realized when I reflect on that day.

Let me give you an example with the lady on the wing holding the baby. I was the last passenger off the plane that day. I wasn't planning on that, but it just happened that way for a number of reasons. When I was holding onto the door and holding onto the life raft, I saw the lady holding a baby. She was in a total uncertain state. She was traumatized.

All my training told me I had to get her to a certain state to get her to move, because if she didn't move everybody behind her on the wing, including me, was not going to get off this plane. It was going to be a tragic situation. I used the technique of startling her. I yelled at her and said, "Throw the baby, throw the baby." No woman is going to throw her baby, but what happened was I got her attention and I broke her state. All of a sudden, she looked at me, someone with certainty, and another lady who was nearby picked up on that cue and said, "Give me the baby." Suddenly, she was in a certain state because her baby was going to be taken care of. She gave that lady her baby, got on the lifeboat, and people were able to walk down the wing.

That was a real telling moment about how to manage somebody's certainty when they're in an uncertain state. People will follow people who are the most certain.

Create Your Own Flight Plan
Exercise

- What lessons have you learned in your life that have prepared you for a situation where you needed certainty?
- What is the earliest memory that you have of when you were absolutely certain? How did that make you feel?
- What are you currently absolutely certain about?
- Where are you currently lacking certainty? What can you do to gain more certainty?
- Think of a time when you were in an uncomfortable situation. What did you do to step up as a leader?
- What are some techniques you use to feel certain?

"People will follow the person who exhibits and exudes the most certainty."
–Dave Sanderson

Next Steps
Contact me at http://davesandersonspeaks.com/contact-us/ to get a complimentary video from my upcoming video series, *Create Your Own Flight Plan.*

|4| RESPONSIVENESS

"We need to try to do the right thing every time,
to perform at our best because we never know what
moment in our lives we'll be judged on."
–Chesley B. "Sully" Sullenberger, III

US Airways Flight 1549 Timeline

3:25 pm Flight 1549 departed from LaGuardia Airport

3:27 pm Bird strike, airplane lost thrust in both engines

3:31 pm Flight 1549 landed in the Hudson River

3:35 pm First ferry arrived to rescue passengers and crew

It was about three and a half minutes from the time the birds hit the plane to the time Captain Sullenberger said the words, "Brace for impact," and the plane was in the water.

The first ferry arrived within four minutes. Within four minutes of landing in the icy Hudson River, commuter ferryboats arrived, along with the Coast Guard and the police.

As soon as the plane touched down in the water, radar and tower personnel notified the Coast Guard, who responded, "We launched the fleet."

Within five minutes, all 155 people on board the plane were safe.

In A Matter Of Moments

Ten months after the events of that day, I was on *The Oprah Winfrey Show* with the flight crew, 82 other passengers, and some of the first responders. Oprah used a statement I made in an interview that the real heroes of the day were the first responders.

One thing I learned about the first responders is how they showed up, not only quickly, but how they focused on what we needed. It wasn't about what they needed. That was a great lesson, a great metaphor. When you're in a crisis situation with someone, you've got to disassociate and you've got to be able to focus on what that other person needs at that moment in time.

Each one of us had a different need. Some people didn't get injured at all. Some people were home within two hours. Some of us went to the triage center. Some of us stayed in the hospital. Everybody had a different need.

In terms of Responsiveness, there are two things that really stand out to me. Number one, the ability for the first responders to respond how they did was massive. The second is how people responded while we were on the plane.

Check Your Ego at the Door

One of the biggest takeaways for me from the "Miracle on the Hudson" is how people checked their egos at the door and responded to other people's needs. You would think, and maybe you've seen this in movies, where people go crazy; they're fighting over seats and knocking people over in order to get off the plane. That didn't happen. One of the greatest lessons I learned about responsiveness is that sometimes you have to check your ego at the door. You have to let other people do what they do best. Some people did exactly what they were told: they followed instructions and immediately exited the plane. Some people stayed back. Some people helped other people, such as a lady with her mother in the back who needed help getting off the plane. Seeing how people respond in crisis situations, especially with a plane crash, you realize how important this one skill is.

People responded to Captain Sullenberger when he clearly said, "Brace for impact." And when we were getting off the plane, it wasn't chaotic. There was a controlled chaos. People responded to each other, and everyone had their own common outcome, but everybody was respectful. I think that was one of the biggest takeaways for me – people checked their ego's at the door. If anybody had not responded, and there were opportunities not to, there could have been a lot more tragedy on that plane.

Let Go Of Judgment

There was a situation where a lady, who was already outside of the plane, returned inside to get her luggage. I was hanging out the door on the other side of the plane, and I heard something going on behind me, so I looked back in. I saw this lady getting her luggage. She was pulling her luggage up the aisle, and I started yelling at her. Another person on the other side of the plane also started yelling at her, and all of a sudden, she's pulling it up and we got her out the door. We got her on the lifeboat. She dropped her purse. I got her purse, threw it back at her, makeup's floating all over the place.

One thing it taught me was that everybody responds in a different way. In times of crisis, you respond to what's most valuable to you, whether it's your life, your kids, whatever it may be. For the lady on the wing, it was her baby, but for this lady, it was obviously her luggage for some reason. It was a great lesson because Captain Sullenberger wrote about this in his book; you think a basic lesson of plane crashes is once you're off the plane you don't go back in. You don't know how people think, how they're going to respond, and you can't judge people.

That was a great lesson for my life. I was probably pretty judgmental of people, but I don't blame myself because I think everybody has done it. After the plane crash, I realized I can't judge people. I don't know what their back story is, I don't know where they came from, I don't know what resources they have or don't have. I don't know what their whole story is.

Responsiveness In Leadership

Years earlier, I learned another valuable lesson regarding responsiveness. I graduated from James Madison University in 1983, found a job, but I quickly realized that it wasn't my passion. I really didn't want to live in Washington, DC so I moved home. My father gave me the "talk" that went something like: you have three weeks to find a job and find an apartment to live in. When three weeks passed and I had not found a job, he called a friend who was a regional manager with Howard Johnson's. I had an interview and was hired as a manager trainee. I learned a lot from that experience, skills I still use to this day. At first, I thought the job was something that was not to my personal liking, but I had a job and I was out of my dad's house. I initially gave into the thought process that this was going to be my destiny, but in life, sometimes you don't know how things will ultimately work out. Coach Lou Holtz said, "You don't really know how the outcome will be until the entire game is played." I was single and moving around to different stores not making much money.

About three years after I started with Howard Johnson's, the restaurant division was purchased by Marriott Corporation. As this was going on, I got engaged to my wife, Terri. She was incredibly supportive as she would travel from Charlotte, North Carolina to see me at whatever store I was working in. The last store I was assigned to with Marriott was in Vienna, Virginia. My next move would have been either Baltimore or Philadelphia for the same amount of money I was making, moving me further away from Charlotte and from Terri. That didn't sit too well with my future wife, so ultimately, I made the decision to leave Marriott and move back to Charlotte.

As I was working out the final months of my assignment with Marriott, I was the first assistant manager, second in charge of the store, which meant I worked most afternoons and nights. It was Christmas Eve and right after lunch. The store was located across the road from the Tysons Corner Center mall. The store filled up quickly when we were preparing to restock and clean. We were understaffed and I was running from the front of the house to the back of the house, covering wherever I was needed. As I was moving from back of house to front of house, I looked up and saw a contingent of well-dressed men in suits and I recognized one of them; it was Bill Marriott, the CEO of Marriott Corporation. He and his management team were out visiting stores. I didn't know what to do so I went up to him and introduced myself as the manager on duty. He looked around and asked me if everything was alright. I told him yes, and then he asked me if I needed any help. I quickly evaluated how to answer; do I say no and have him see that everything is not alright and I'm over my head, or do I say yes and have him think that I am not the guy for the job? I quickly decided to tell him yes, I could use some help in the back of the house with dropping fries. He quickly moved toward the kitchen, but before he got there, he turned to his team and told them to jump in. They started to bus tables for me while the CEO of Marriott dropped fries. It taught me a tremendous lesson about leadership and being responsive. When all heck is breaking loose, you realize that you are not too big or important to not help out and respond to the moment. I later realized that Mr. Marriott knew that his name was on the building, and ultimately, the company's success or failure depended on pulling together as a team and responding to the customer. This was as much as his responsibility as it was mine or the waitress in front. It was my first major lesson on how responsiveness is a key trait of a good leader.

Responsiveness: A Key Skill

The lesson from that day in the restaurant has served as a tremendous model for me. As I grew my career into sales and established my own organization, I always incorporated a "responsiveness plan" into how I conducted my business. Building and reinforcing responsiveness is critical to long-term success in any business. Demonstrating that your motives to support someone quickly are genuine and congruent is the most effective way to build and reinforce responsiveness. Once your potential client sees that you have their best interests at heart, you will become their trusted advisor instead of just another commodity. Being responsive is a key attribute that determines the difference between being a vendor or being a partner. In my organization, we integrate responsiveness into everything we do. Although there are thousands of speakers who do what I do, one of the reasons my business keeps growing is because my team and I respond rapidly to client requests. This helps demonstrate that we have their interests at heart. Another way we respond to a client's needs is to go the extra mile by asking, "How can we add more value to your experience than you expect?" Sometimes our clients have needs that even they don't realize, the need for congruency. If you work and live with congruency – a trait lacking in most organizations – you will stand out from your competition.

Create Your Own Flight Plan
Keys to Responsiveness

- Demonstrate that your motives are genuine and congruent
- Don't judge another person's response to a situation
- Go the extra mile by asking your clients or customers, "How can we add more value to your experience than you expect?"

"Check the ego at the door and
serve from the heart and
all will fall into place."
–Dave Sanderson

Next Steps

Contact me at http://davesandersonspeaks.com for monthly updates on my webcast series, *Create your own Flight Plan!*

|5| STATE MANAGEMENT

"You have the power over your mind –
not outside events.
Realize this, and you will find strength."
–Marcus Aurelius

Recently, I spoke to a group of women entrepreneurs. During the question and answer portion of my presentation, a lady asked, "How does somebody really manage their mind through a crisis?" I shared with them something I learned in 1994 from Tony Robbins, and I employed it that day in the plane crash. If you've been to any of Tony Robbins' events, the first thing he talks about is the way to manage your state, which is another way of saying the way you manage your mind.

There are three ways to do this:

1. By changing the way you move or your physiology;

2. By changing what you focus on; or

3. By changing how you speak to yourself and the language patterns that you use.

Several years ago, I had the honor to spend time with Tony at his Namale Resort in Fiji. We were on our way to go jump off a bridge into a natural salt river in the middle of the night. The distance between the bridge and the river is pretty significant. However, once you get the courage to jump, you land in the warm water and float in the darkness, under the stars, where you eventually end up in a beautiful salt water lagoon. On our way to the bridge, and anticipating the jump we were about to experience, we were talking about how to manage your mind when your mind starts questioning things. Tony said, "You've got to put yourself in a state of resourcefulness and gratitude. You've got to do it radically with a change of physiology, focus, or how you talk to yourself."

Once we reached the bridge, where I could not see anything below me, and it was my time to jump I realized I had to change my focus. I changed my focus at that moment from fear of the unknown to gratitude for being there to experience this magical opportunity, and I jumped. This is a lesson that I have used consistently when I have those moments when I really start to question myself.

That day on the plane when we were going down, I had one of those moments. After Captain Sullenberger crossed over the George Washington Bridge and I said my final prayers, I remembered that day on the bridge in Fiji, in the dark, having to summon the gratitude before I jumped into the salt river, not knowing the outcome. How I felt that day in Fiji was eerily similar to January 15, 2009. I remembered what Tony told me that night and in those last moments before we crashed, I wasn't scared, and I got what he meant when I felt that moment of gratitude.

After we crashed, I had to radically change my state. I did this by changing the way I was speaking to myself and the way I was focusing. I was now focusing on the outcome and talking to myself about how I had to be resourceful, how I had to figure things out, and how I had to do things.

Then my mother started talking to me about if I did the right thing, I'd be ok. I employed that one skill from 1994 that I learned from Tony and which he reinforced when we were in Fiji, not only to save myself that day, but hopefully help other people in a time of crisis. Next time you find yourself in a challenging situation, just remember the basics.

State management, I believe, was the distinguishing factor in why this day turned out the way it did. Everybody on that plane managed their state in a lot of different ways. First, Captain Sullenberger had to manage his state through focus. I don't know if you heard the flight recorder rendition, but the first thing that he did was to say, "My plane." He used it to change the state immediately through his language pattern, but then it was all focus, and through the entire time from getting that plane over the bridge to the Hudson River, he managed through focus.

Other people on the plane managed it differently. One was a lady. As we were going down, I heard two things. The first thing was the flight attendant saying, "Brace, brace, brace." The second was a lady in the back saying the Lord's Prayer, and I believe she was managing her state through faith and through her language patterns. That's how she had to get her proper state of whatever was going to happen to her. She had to do it through her language patterns by saying the Lord's Prayer and through faith.

One of the amazing things about this experience for me is understanding how a similar experience for all of us resulted in so many different perspectives and how people manage their states so differently. Let me share some examples.

I had the opportunity to be on *Good Morning America* a few years ago with a number of different passengers from Flight 1549. There was one gentleman from the plane who was on the show that day with us. After we were finished, we were all talking and sharing experiences. He basically said to us all, "I don't want to ever see you people again. This has been a horrible experience for me. I may lose my job. I don't know why I went through this and I don't ever want to see you people again." He went into a depressed state.

In the same situation that I had, last year I was interviewed by *AARP The Magazine* about why I took the pathway that I did. I said, "It's because I asked a different question." My question was: *How can I add even more value to people?* Therefore, I took this experience as a positive pathway, an opportunity to impact people.

One way that I help other people in business situations change their state is by asking them a different level of question. I learned two questions back in the early 1990s that all of a sudden changed the direction of my sales career where I was making money, I was doing all right, but I was never excelling. I asked these two questions and everything started changing with it. All of a sudden, I was in alignment with my client. The questions were:

- "What's most important to you?" and

- "What has to happen for you to be able to realize that?"

Once I started asking people those two questions in my first or second meeting with them, my sales improved. I ask those two questions in every transaction, every company I'm ever involved with, and that's why I went from a commodity to having raving fans and repeat business. In sales, especially financial services, it's all about repeat business.

One of the biggest instances when one has to help somebody else manage their state is after the loss of a loved one. When my father passed away, I had to help manage the estate which I had never done before. During a highly emotional time is the moment when you have to manage your state and everybody else's states. One of the things that helped me was his financial advisor from Wells Fargo. He said, "Listen. We're going to get through this, and I'm going to help you get through this." He really put me in a calm state. All of a sudden, he helped me make some decisions that had to be made, and he had my father's best interests at heart. I knew that, so he had my best interests at heart, too.

Over the years I've had my money in multiple places and with different companies, but after I saw how he performed for me and my family, I put all my money with him. He turned me into a raving fan out of a tragedy. The one thing he did was he got to my heart. In sales, if you can understand those two questions, what's most important and what has to happen for them to get that, you then understand what's in that person's heart. All of a sudden, you can help at a different level and now you can make them a raving fan.

In fact, I'm still with the same insurance person today I was with back in the 1980s, because he made me a raving fan of his because he always checks in. He's responsive. He gives me certainty that he's going to do the right thing.

When Tony Robbins teaches the three different ways to change people's states through their physiology, their language patterns, and the way they focus, all those things can be accomplished whether you're on the phone, in person, or talking through video. So remember, the next time you engage with somebody, understand what state they're in at that moment. If they're in the appropriate state to communicate, great. But if they're not, help them get into a more appropriate state by changing the way they move, asking them a question by helping them focus on something a little bit different, and then you'll be able to help them and add even more value to their life.

Create Your Own Flight Plan
Review – State Management

1. Physiology: how do you manage your body to get yourself in a proper state of mind? The way you move, the gestures that you make.

2. Focus: what you're focusing on in the moment can determine how you're thinking, and how you're going to feel.

3. Language patterns. How do you speak to yourself internally and externally? Some people have negative thoughts: "Why can't I do this? Why am I doing this? Why is this always happening to me?" which puts them in a depressed state. Instead, they could ask more empowering questions: "What do I have to do to get X?" which is a different level of question.

"Once you can manage your state,
you can help people step up."
–Dave Sanderson

Next Steps

Check out my new video series, *The 10 Key Strategies Tony Robbins taught me to compress decades into days*, at http://davesandersonspeaks.com/contact-us/

"What lies before us

and what lies behind us are small matters

compared to what lies within us."

–Henry David Thoreau

|6| SENSORY ACUITY AND COMMUNICATION

> "The world is full of magic things, patiently
> waiting for our senses to grow sharper."
> –W. B. Yeats

Sensory Acuity

The capacity to be **acutely** aware through our **senses**
Seeing – Visual
Hearing – Auditory
Touching/Feeling – Kinesthetic
Taste – Gustatory
Smell - Olfactory

That day, after we landed in the Hudson River, one of the key skills that I used to help me and other people was my ability to understand people's senses. What I mean by that is this: sensory acuity is one of the key skills that people use, whether you're in a visual mode or an auditory mode or a kinesthetic mode. Everybody goes to that key modality that they live in when it's a fight or flight response. That day on the plane, I was a visual person, so I really visually understood what was going on, but some people were in an auditory mode, and you had to actually speak to them to get their attention. That's why, next time, when you're in a situation where you have to make an important decision, get in your primary mode – whether it's visual, auditory, or kinesthetic – understand what that is, and at that point, you'll be able to make a decision to get the job done.

Everybody's got a primary sense, or modality, that they use. Hint: if you don't know what your primary modality is, ask your partner, your parents, or your closest friends.

Using Sensory Acuity to Improve Relationships

I'll give the example of my wife and myself. We've been married for almost 30 years. It took me many years to realize that my wife is purely auditory. She wants to be heard. She loves to talk and she loves to be able to communicate in an auditory manner, while I'm a visual person. You show me something, and 15 seconds later, I've got it. Let's move on. I don't need to have a 30-minute conversation about what's going on. Just tell me. Once I learned that when I'm communicating with my wife I had to listen for 30 minutes before I could say a word, our relationship improved. Because if you interrupt an auditory person, they hate it because they don't think that you have been listening to them, even though you have heard everything that they have said.

Once I realized that, it changed every way I communicated with my wife. Then I identified the primary sense that each one of my kids used. It helped me with my relationships with them, too.

By understanding that people communicate in different modalities, I was able to improve my sensory acuity and communicate with them much better. I can adapt and be resourceful by changing which modality I want to communicate in. I can choose whether I want to communicate in my primary modality (visual) or communicate in their modality, like when I'm having a conversation with my wife who is auditory.

Using Sensory Acuity in Business

Understanding sensory acuity has not only changed everything in my personal life, but in my business life, too. When I go to a business meeting, I quickly understand how that person communicates by their language patterns. They might say, "I hear something" (auditory), or "I see something" (visual), or "I feel something" (kinesthetic). Once I figure that out, I'm able to communicate at their level. We are in sync, we have a rapport. This happened that day on the plane by how I communicated and how other people communicated.

Sensory acuity is a great tool to use not only for communication, but also as a way to grow your business. In my workshops, I do exercises to help people identify the primary modality they gravitate towards, enabling them to have better relationships with their loved ones, their colleagues, and their customers. I first presented this workshop when I was hired to do a project for Disneyland several years ago. I did a modality assessment of each character and of the different areas of the amusement park, and trained their employees on how to assess other people's modalities quickly.

What I Saw After we Landed in the Hudson

On the plane, once I saw the fire, until the moment we crashed, I was in a visual state. I was also seeing everything that passed through my mind, what happened in my life up to that point. You read books or hear stories about people who have faced death seeing their whole life pass before their eyes. They call it "The Movie of Your Life." That's exactly what happened to me and some other people I talked to later who were on the plane. While I didn't give up hope, I was resolved that if I didn't survive, I lived a good life. And then all of a sudden, I saw everything, I saw "The Movie of My Life." I was in a very visual mode at that point. I wasn't emotional. I didn't get emotional at all, because I knew where I was going if something did happen.

I was at peace, but I was sad at the same time. I wondered if my wife would do what I told her to do if anything were to happen to me. That was my last thought before we hit the water. *Was my wife going to do what I told her to do?* I told her to pay off the house and pay off the kids' college education. Then we crashed and I came back up. I looked out the window. I was once again back in the visual mode, because once I realized I didn't break any bones and I was alive, I had to really analyze, "Okay, how the hell am I going to get out of here?"

I looked around, and even though water was filling up the plane immediately, which was at 36° Fahrenheit with ice, I didn't feel it. Once you go to a certain modality, you tend to stay in that modality. Everything else goes away. I didn't hear anything going on. I saw people get on top of the seats. They walked on top of them. I saw people moving. I didn't listen to anything. I was focused on looking around to determine, "How am I going to get out of here?"

When people go into a crisis situation, they go to their primary modality. For me, it's visual. Some people were auditory. Some people on the plane had to yell to get other passengers to move, and they had to go into an auditory modality by yelling. I talked with some of the people on the plane later, who said they smelled the birds burning in the engines (olfactory). I didn't smell anything, but I took their word for it.

Even when I jumped into the river and swam from the plane to the ferry, I didn't feel the water. I was still in visual mode. It wasn't until I reached the ferry and realized I couldn't climb the ladder to safety that I switched to auditory. I yelled up to the people on the ferry, "I can't climb. I can't." Then I heard what my mom used to say to me when I was growing up, "If you can't, you must. If you can't do it, you must do it." Two men reached down and pulled me out of the water onto the boat.

As that day progressed, I think people stayed in their primary mode until they had to change. That's what happened to me.

People have five primary senses: sight, hearing, taste, smell, and touch. The ability to understand a person's primary modality is a key driver in having a resource available to be able to communicate more effectively.

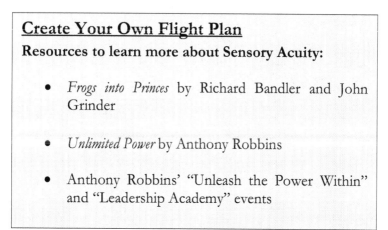

<u>Create Your Own Flight Plan</u>
Resources to learn more about Sensory Acuity:

- *Frogs into Princes* by Richard Bandler and John Grinder

- *Unlimited Power* by Anthony Robbins

- Anthony Robbins' "Unleash the Power Within" and "Leadership Academy" events

"**Speak in such a way
that others love to listen to you.
Listen in such a way
that others love to speak to you.**"
–Anon

<u>Next Steps</u>
If you are looking for a speaker for your audience who is uniquely positioned to not only inspire but share skillsets that some of the top leaders in the world use to make a difference in their business and people's lives, please go to:
http://davesandersonspeaks.com/contact-us/

|7| FOCUS

**"Always remember,
your focus determines your reality."
–George Lucas**

"If you could have any superpower what would it be?" I was asked this question during a recent podcast interview. I replied, "The ability to focus immediately on the outcome."

The reason is that having laser-focus, and not allowing external factors and noise to distract you, can significantly fast-track the achievement of any outcome. If I had been laser-focused on achieving my mission, the path that I have taken since the plane crash would have been very different.

Doing the Right Thing

Back in 2009, there was a directional change, not only in my life but also in where my career was going. It wasn't by design that I was the last passenger off of the plane that day; it just worked out that way. I heard my mother's voice saying, "If you do the right thing, God will take care of you." To me, "doing the right thing" meant helping other people first. That is why I got off the plane last. I wanted to make sure people from the back of the plane got off so I was the last passenger to disembark. From there, the route I took was also different. In order to get off the plane, I had to swim to the ferryboat. By this point, I was suffering from hypothermia, and my body was so cold that I could not get myself onto the ferry without help. I was no longer in a place where I was able to help anyone else; I was the one who needed help. Having just faced the possibility of death, I started to realize that my life wasn't focused on what it should be. I wasn't there for my own family a lot of the time. I was concentrating on trying to earn a living and make money so I could give them everything they wanted, but I was missing a lot. I wasn't there when my kids probably really needed me to be. I was selfishly trying to build my career instead of being there for my family.

In the hospital that night, the only person who called me was Tony Robbins. My company didn't call to check in on me. In fact, they didn't even call my wife, which was even worse. The next day, when I arrived back home in Charlotte, I stopped by the office. I was still wearing the sweat suit that the Red Cross volunteer brought me the night before. I went there so they could see that I was still alive. My regional manager looked at me and said, "You are going on that business trip next week right?" I didn't know what to say. I did go on that business trip, but it was a rough ride.

Brace for Impact

The following year we released our book *Brace for Impact*. I was a contributing author along with several other passengers from Flight 1549. We did some interviews in New York to promote the book. I was with two other passengers, sharing stories from the last several months. One guy described about how his company responded immediately after the crash: "My company came with a private plane, flew me back home, and I got a couple weeks of time off. They took great care of me." One of woman said that her company's CEO flew his private plane to New York, brought her back to Atlanta, and told her to take as much time as she needed. When it was my turn to share, all I could say was: "They didn't even check on me, and they asked me to go back to work the next week." That's when I realized my focus needed to change. What I was doing was no longer working for me.

Becoming an Entrepreneur

My initiation as a professional speaker happened the week after the crash when I was asked to speak at my church. It went well. A little while later, I had the opportunity to speak for the American Red Cross in front of a very large group in Charlotte. I was amazed at how well they responded to my story. I think everybody should have a mission, and part of mine is to help the Red Cross raise money and get those much-needed funds to assist in local and national emergencies. Somebody heard me speak at that event and asked me to speak at another event, which was filmed. That film was posted online, and some people in Washington, DC saw it. They invited me to speak at a national event. That turned into another invitation, and I was asked if I'd be interested in speaking at future events. That's how I started to grow my speaking side-job while still working for my former company.

During the five years after the "Miracle on the Hudson," I had spoken so much and had met many entrepreneurs that inspired me to start looking at a bigger picture—not only for me but, really, for my family. That gave me the direction and motivation I needed to start taking control of my own destiny and leave the corporate job I was in.

The one thing Tony would say to me every time I would see

him over the course of ten years was, "Dave, are you working for yourself yet? Why are you still working for somebody else? Work for yourself; you can make it." And I kept telling him, "I'm not ready yet. I need to make money. I need to get this. I need to get that." I always had excuses. And that doesn't fly with Tony; you can't give him excuses. He doesn't deal with them very well. I finally realized I had to do it. It was time, and he coached me through that period.

I made the decision to go full-fledged into a speaking and coaching business. Yes, there were going to be some challenges. There are always challenges; there are always risks, but the way I look at it is I survived the plane crash in ice-cold water. I was blessed to be able to do that. So any time things get tough, I have a reference for my faith to be able to get me through it. Now I can be there for my family and focus on building a life instead of just working in a career.

For a long time I was stuck in a rut where I didn't have a clear mission. My mission was to make money, to make sure my kids and family were taken care of. That's not a big enough mission, and I think that day on the Hudson allowed me to realize that I survived for a different purpose—not to just go back to working for somebody who may or may not care about me. My focus changed. I realized I wanted to change people's lives. That's the bigger mission.

Fortunately for me, it wasn't too late. The "Miracle on the Hudson" taught me to slow down and be there for my family, and now I have a tremendous relationship with my kids. I no longer only schedule business events; I also schedule family events and make it a priority to be at every one. By changing my focus, I changed my life.

Create Your Own Flight Plan
Exercise

- What area of your life needs your focus?

- Write down three actions you can take to improve your focus in this area.

- Identify a friend who could support you become more focused in this area.

"If you don't make the time to work on creating the life you want, you're going to be forced to spend a lot of time dealing with a life you don't want."
–Kevin Ngo

Next Steps
If you are an aspiring speaker and need professional assistance to get your platform up and running quickly and seamlessly, contact Denise Griffitts at http://yourofficeontheweb.com/contact/. Please tell her I sent you!

"If you want your life and work to be meaningful, then focus on the things that matter most and spend your time, efforts and resources on those things that ARE meaningful."

–Andrey Sergeyev

|8| ANTICIPATION

"A good hockey player plays where the puck is.
A great hockey player plays
where the puck is going to be."
– Wayne Gretzky

What will matter most to you in the end? If you were suddenly faced with the possibility of dying, what would you do with the time you had left? If you knew your time was short, what would be most important to you?

When we passed over the George Washington Bridge on Flight 1549, I started to anticipate what the potential outcomes could be, and none of them were very optimistic. In fact, in anticipation of not making it, I put my wallet inside my pants so that my body could be identified. Thankfully, I was wrong.

Have a Game Plan

When we landed in the Hudson River, I knew my game plan, which was to get out of the plane as fast as possible. But as soon as I hit the aisle, I heard my mom's voice say, "If you do the right thing, God will take care of you," and my game plan changed. The ability to anticipate my other options was a key resource that I used that day.

As a young boy growing up in Southwest Ohio, I was a huge

Boston Celtics fan. There was a team in Cincinnati, the Royals, and I enjoyed going to their games with my dad, but there was something magical about the Celtics. More specifically, there was something magical about John Havlicek. John grew up in Ohio and attended Ohio State, but that wasn't what made me a fan. It was the way he played—and, more importantly—the way he anticipated everyone's next move.

John was a huge part of the Celtics dynasty. He was never the one who stood out in the stats, but he changed the game every time he stepped on the court. As I grew up, I patterned my game, whether it was basketball, football, or baseball, on John Havlicek's. John was the guy who was able to read a situation and be one step ahead of the play. He never stopped moving, which made playing against him difficult.

As I grew up playing sports, I learned how to do the same thing. My coaches would often get upset with me because I was the guy who anticipated the next play and disrupted it before it could be practiced. I ultimately learned how to incorporate my skill into the practices so that I didn't disrupt preparations for the game. However, in actual games, this skill often helped me make game-changing plays, whether it was anticipating a tipoff, seeing what a base-runner would do next, or predicting the next play the offense would run.

In 1976, I had the opportunity to attend the Gale Catlett basketball camp in Cincinnati. At that time, I was living in Winchester, Virginia, but our coach was a big Gale Catlett fan, and he took a few of us to the camp. At that camp, I was on the championship team, and one of the perks was getting to play 1-on-1 with the big "O," Oscar Robertson. I was a huge fan of Oscar's, and it was quite an honor to not only meet him, but also play against him. Oscar talked while we were playing in front of the camp. I had seen Oscar play often when I was in Ohio, so as he was backing me into the basket, I anticipated his signature move, backside in, stepped out to shoot, and stole the ball from him. He smiled and told me no one in the NBA could do that! This made my dad's day, but, more importantly, it taught me an important lesson that I have used in every venture I have been involved with—the skill of anticipation is something that can not only help you stand out, but also help you overcome challenging times.

Using Anticipation in Business

If I had to point to one skill that helped me grow and become a top producer in whatever I did, it would be the skill of anticipation. In sales, I made many mistakes, but when I relied on my instincts and built relationships with prospective clients, I was able to anticipate the best way to serve them at the most important times. This took me from an average producer to a top producer in every company I was with.

When I worked with the security team for Tony Robbins, Tony told me that the one skill he valued most in his team was the skill of anticipation. When I was with him, one of the reasons he and I got along so well was that I could anticipate his next move. I had the power to understand what was important to him next. Anticipation is something I practice with pretty much everybody in my life, whether it's my family, my business partners, or my friends. What will they need next? I try to get in front of that, and through this strategy, I'm able to gain instant rapport. Then, I'm looking out for them, and not for me.

I've often heard Tony share a story about his meeting with Wayne Gretzky. What made Wayne the best hockey player was the way he always knew where the puck was going, not just where it was. Tony said that mastering the skill of anticipation was what separates someone from being able to manage people to being able to lead people.

That day, on Flight 1549, the ability to anticipate was a skill that Captain Sullenberger used to make his decisions on how and where to go. He had to anticipate that we couldn't return to LaGuardia Airport or make it to Teterboro Airport in time. The ferries had to anticipate that something was wrong and change their direction to be there to assist.

Anticipation was a primary skill that saved the day not only for me, but for all of us. If I hadn't watched and learned what I did when I was young from people like John Havlicek, that day and my life may have had a very different outcome.

All of the moments in your life do matter. You never know which moments will make a real difference. President Clinton said that the moment he met President Kennedy when he was in college was the moment he knew he had a different pathway. I believe that everyone has that seminal moment in their life. Some people take the next step toward action, and some people don't. When that moment happens to you, it may determine your destiny.

Create Your Own Flight Plan
Increase Your Ability to Anticipate

- **Start with what you know:** The more you know, the better you can respond and predict. Learn more about who and what is around you. Pay attention, and you'll notice clues.
- **Think in "What Ifs":** Think through scenarios. Consider, "What if I did X?" Then identify some potential results. Think about how each choice you make impacts your next choice. This strategy will give you a great perspective that will enable future anticipation.
- **Think it through:** Slow down, consider all of your options, and think through the possibilities. People who are in a hurry often overlook opportunities to be proactive and anticipate accordingly.
- **Be aware:** One of the best ways to anticipate is to pay attention. Notice what is going on around you, weigh your options, and then respond.

"Anticipate the difficult by managing the easy."
–Lao Tzu

Next Steps

Sign up to get my newsletter at
http://davesandersonspeaks.com. Use the code "offer" and I'll send you a complimentary copy of my book *HalfTime*!

"Anticipation is the heart of wisdom.
If you are going to cross a desert,
you anticipate that you will be thirsty,
and you take water."
–Mark Helprin

|9| RISK ASSESSMENT

"Let me not pray to be sheltered from dangers,
but to be fearless in facing them.
Let me not beg for the stilling of my pain,
but for the heart to conquer it."
—Rabindranath Tagore

After I heard the explosion while sitting in seat 15A, I looked out the window and saw fire coming out from underneath the left wing. I didn't know at the time that a flock of Canadian geese had collided with our plane, which had caused the loud explosion. That's the moment I started to assess all the different risks that I may have, which included not only getting off the plane, but hopefully surviving the initial plane crash.

The ability to assess risk, especially in a time of a crisis, and keep your mind about you is one of the key reasons that I survived the plane crash of Flight 1549.

As we crossed over the George Washington Bridge and I clearly saw people's faces who were on the bridge, I knew something bad was probably about to happen. I started assessing my risks very quickly, but one thing you realize when you're going down in a plane about to crash is that you don't have much control over anything except your mind. So in those final seconds before it crashed, I was assessing the risk of, if I survived, how I was going to get out of the plane.

Once we got down and ultimately came to a stop, I immediately started to execute that plan.

An Early Life Lesson

Assessing risk was a lesson I began to learn at an early age. When I was in Boy Scouts, I was focused on becoming an Eagle Scout. In the town I grew up in – Hillsboro, Ohio – only one scout had attained that rank at that time. He was our troop leader, Lawson Walker, and he was a great role model for being a Boy Scout. He took me under his wing and I followed every piece of advice he gave me about being a Scout. He told me that one way to progress towards achieving Eagle Scout was to get my "Order of the Arrow" (OA) award. Since it was founded in 1915, the OA has recognized Scouts and Scouters who best exemplify the Scout Oath and Law in their daily lives. This recognition provides encouragement for others to live by these ideals as well. I was selected to go for this distinction when I was 12 years old. One thing I realized when I arrived for the OA weekend adventure was that I didn't know anyone there. My dad dropped me off and I was on my own. It was one of my first recollections of being dropped off by myself, not knowing anyone, and having to figure things out for myself. Over the weekend, we were constantly moving, doing tasks along the way with no sleep, and were given a specific time frame to finish all tasks. Many were fun tasks but had an element of danger to them, such as spelunking in a cave, climbing a rocky side of a large hill, swimming across a river with all your gear. For each task, I had to assess the risks and rely on strangers to accomplish them. I admit there were times when I questioned my decision to go for this distinction because I was uncomfortable relying on people with whom I had no connection, but I had to have faith in my abilities and trust that I had made the right decision. At the end of the trek, we had a limited amount of time to carve an arrow out of a log, which would designate that we had made it. This OA weekend adventure was the first time I remember being put in a position to constantly assess risk. I ultimately earned the rank of Order of the Arrow, and it was one of the most important weekends of my life. It gave me a solid life reference and the certainty that when put to the task, I could make the right decisions about risks.

How to Assess Risk

As I got older, my dad reinforced the importance of the ability to assess risk. In fact, he taught me something a long time ago that really played into how I responded that day on the plane.

When it comes to evaluating risks:

1. You have to assess and identify the risk: is it a good risk or a bad risk to take?

2. You have to assess and identify the exit strategy for anything you get into.

The truth is, I didn't really understand what he meant by this until I purchased my first car. I was 22 years old and I traded in my first car that my dad had given me to buy a sporty Datsun 280ZX. My dad asked me how I was going to get out of the car – my exit strategy – and how much the insurance was going to cost me. Of course, I hadn't thought about these things. I was 22 years old and just happy to have a car.

Once I assessed them, I learned important lessons. First, I have to assess the risks of anything I get into. Second, I have to have an exit strategy on how to get out.

Risk Balance: Deposits and Withdrawals

These two lessons actually played into that day on Flight 1549 a lot. As our plane was heading over the George Washington Bridge straight into the Hudson River, all of us had to assess the potential risks and quickly put an action plan together in the event we got down successfully. Captain Sullenberger had to assess the risks of the options he had. Should he try to return to LaGuardia? How does Teterboro Airport look as an option? Can he really go into the Hudson River, miss every obstacle in the way, and land it so we had a chance to survive? In six minutes, he had to assess the potential risks and make a call. I had many different moments to assess what pathways I may have to get out of the plane. What if I was injured? What if I was under water? Do I help others first or head out? When I got to the door and there was no room on the wing or boat for me, what do I do? When I felt the plane sinking, do I try and swim with all my clothes on? There were many risks we had to assess quickly, just like when I was 12 and going for my Order of the Arrow. I knew no one on the plane that day. I was put in a position to perform many potentially life-threatening tasks, and I had to rely on others to make the correct decisions so I could survive. I had to swim with all my clothes on in a moving river, just like when I was 12. All moments in your life matter. When you are put in a specific situation in life that you may think is meaningless, that one moment may determine your destiny. Captain Sullenberger has said on many occasions, "For 42 years I had made small, regular deposits of education, training, and experience. And the experience balance was sufficient that on January 15, I could make a sudden, large withdrawal." It was the same for me and I'm guessing for everyone on that plane that day. The ability to assess risk and take the appropriate action is one of the most important resources you need in your life.

The next time you get in a challenging situation, remember – assess your risk quickly. Identify whether it's a good risk or a bad risk to take and determine your exit strategy. Start making decisions about what you're going to do, and then stick to that plan, execute that plan, because ultimately once you have the conviction and belief that your plan's going to work, you have a better chance of making sure it does.

Create Your Own Flight Plan
Exercise

- What areas of your life need to be evaluated/risk assessed?
- Identify the different areas in your life — relationships, health, spirituality, wealth, career, etc.
- Rank the amount of time you spend in each area vs. the reward you get from doing it.
- What do you notice?
- Are you balanced? Does your life look the way you want it to?
- What would you like to change? How are you going to make those changes?
- What are some resources you can use to take the first steps now towards making a change?

"For 42 years I had made small, regular deposits
of education, training, and experience.
And the experience balance was sufficient
that on January 15, I could make a sudden,
large withdrawal."
–Chesley B. "Sully" Sullenberger, III

Next Steps
If you have a story about survival or strategies that can help others in their business or personal life, please contact me at http://davesandersonspeaks.com/contact-us/

|10| PERSISTENCE

> "Brick walls are there for a reason.
> They let us prove how badly we want things."
> –Dr. Randy Pausch, *The Last Lecture*

I get asked a lot of questions about the "Miracle on the Hudson" and what I experienced that day. One question that comes up a lot is, "What's the one skill that's helped you get to where you're at today?" That one skill that's helped me more than any other is my ability to persist—to hang in there.

Persistence means never giving up. It's always having a strategy for how you're going to do something. You never give up on a strategy until you can't make any more progress. I think life is about making progress.

Persist Until You Achieve Your Outcome

If you've ever been in sales or any management position, you know that people push back on you. People reject you. I've learned that you can't take this personally. You've got to hang in there. You've got to persist until you get your outcome.

This is a lesson that was reinforced every time I spent time with Tony Robbins. Tony teaches that you continue to make progress towards an outcome until it's achieved. I've taken this advice and applied it to everything that I do—not only in sales, but also in my family, in my church, in sports, and in running my first marathon. You have to hang in there and persist until you get the outcome you want.

That day on the plane, if anybody had failed to persist—if they had given up—we would have had a whole different outcome. If I had given up and said, "Once we crash, I'm not going to make it," then I wouldn't be here today. There was a lady in the back of the plane who kept telling everybody, "I'm not going to make it. I'm not going to make it." We all had to give her positive reinforcement to encourage her. We said, "You're going to make it. Just let us help you."

Remember, if you hit a roadblock or need help, there are people out there who will help you persist and help you reach your outcome.

As you're making your goals for the next quarter or the next year and writing down your outcomes, remember: You'll never fail if you don't give up. If you write your goals down, know that you're going to achieve them if you persist until you get your outcome. That's the one thing I do, and that's why I achieve more than 80% of my outcomes every year.

For the 25 years prior to the "Miracle on the Hudson," I was driven to be the best I could be and to provide for my family. That's what my father did when I was growing up, and we turned out pretty well, so it was a model for me to follow. As my wife Terri and I grew our family, I was even more committed to providing for them. This meant that I needed to do more to get the resources we needed. To achieve this, I turned to my personal development mentors. Starting with Earl Nightingale, and continuing with Jim Rohn, Tom Hopkins, Denis Waitley, and, ultimately, Tony Robbins, I invested my time and resources into learning cutting-edge strategies to help me become a sales leader in every company I was with, while also improving my fitness and finances. I was on the right path.

However, as time went on, this rapid and never-ending pace started to take a toll on me personally, emotionally, and in my family life. I knew I had to slow down and change. I knew how to do it, but I had a false belief that if I slowed down, I would never "be all that I could be." All of that changed on January 15, 2009.

After the plane crashed into the Hudson River and I made it out and to the hospital, I found out that my health wasn't as good as I thought it was. I was fit, which is why I was able to swim to the ferry in the 36-degree water, but I wasn't healthy. This was first revealed when I arrived at the triage center, and it was later validated at Palisades Medical Center. If I wanted to be around for a long time, and if I wanted to see all of my kids' graduations and weddings, I had to make a shift.

During those first five hours, when I was in the hospital trying to warm up, I experienced a critical life moment. I was so cold. I could have given up. I could have said, "Is it really worth it? My body is already cold. Let it just go a little colder, and I could just be out of all this pain." But the mindset I grew up with was that you don't give up. You never give up until the last second's off the clock. You just don't give it up.

Never Give Up

This is a message I reinforce when I speak to groups all around the world. I tell them, "You never give up in life." If I had given up, I never would have seen the things that I've since had the opportunity to see. If I had given up, I never could have impacted as many people as I have. If I had given up, you wouldn't be holding this book in your hands.

I've had the honor of visiting places that have faced incredible challenges: Fort Hood after the shootings, Oklahoma after the tornadoes, and the eastern shore of North Carolina after Super Storm Sandy. I've seen tragic situations first-hand. Every time, what I'm most inspired by are the survivors—the people who have lived through tragic situations, but who didn't give up, who persisted.

The 12 resources I've shared with you are all important. But if you don't persist, none of them make any difference. Persistence and the "I'll never give up" mindset are the most important resources you have.

I talk about Tony Robbins a lot, and that's because he's had a tremendous impact on my life. Tony and I are good friends, and I cherish that relationship. But just consider: What if he had given up earlier in life, when he experienced multiple dads, went broke, was overweight, and washed his dishes in the bathtub of his 400-square-foot apartment? What if he had given up when he was told he couldn't do this or that? How many people like me would never have had the opportunity to grow and contribute to society?

Persistence is the most important resource to have if you want to get the most out of this life. Persistence allows you to give back to people and help others. Persistence helps you grow emotionally and become a better person. If you want to contribute to a cause greater than yourself, persistence is key.

Never give up.

Create Your Own Flight Plan
Reminder

- When you make your quarterly or yearly goals, be clear on the outcomes you want to achieve.

- Remember: You'll never fail if you don't give up.

- Write your goals down, and have certainty – know that you're going to achieve them.

- Persist until you get your outcome.

"You have to combine passion and persistence.
You can't give up."
–Dave Sanderson

Next Steps
Every month, I'll be giving a personal tour of US Airways 1549 at the Carolinas Aviation Museum in Charlotte, North Carolina. Sign up for my newsletter at http://davesandersonspeaks.com and use the code "firstinflight" to be considered for this unique opportunity!

"Don't wish it was easier, wish you were better.

Don't wish for less problems, wish for more skills.

Don't wish for less challenge, wish for more wisdom."

–Jim Rohn

|11| TEAMWORK

"The events of January 15, 2009 have been well-
documented, and rather than recite them now in
great detail, I want only to reiterate to the
subcommittee that the successful outcome was
achieved by the actions of many.
Lives were saved due to the combination of a
very experienced, well-trained crew: First Officer
Jeff Skiles, and Flight Attendants Donna Dent,
Doreen Welsh and Sheila Dail,
all of whom acted in a remarkable display of
teamwork, along with expert air traffic
controllers, the orderly cooperation of our cool-
headed passengers, and the quick and
determined actions of the professional and
volunteer first responders in New York City."
–Captain Chesley B. "Sully" Sullenberger
before Congress, February 24, 2009

A while back, I did an interview with a Canadian publication.
They knew that I had been a leader on the Anthony Robbins
Security Team for many years. One of the questions they
asked was: "What attributes of being a leader on the Anthony
Robbins Security Team helped you on January 15, 2009?" I
shared with them that one of the greatest things we did on
the security team was not only to commit to being
outstanding at every event, but also to raise our standards at
every event. By raising our standards, we improved ourselves
and became a better, stronger team. This enabled Tony to do

whatever he needed to do to help people.

Raise Your Standards

Raising your standards simply means turning the things you "should" do (*I should lose weight*) into "musts" (*I will lose weight*). It means creating a plan and following it, no matter what. Turning your "shoulds" into "musts" can change your entire life for the better.

This attribute played out for me on the day of the plane crash. I think Captain Sullenberger and First Officer Skiles did an unbelievable job in getting that plane down safely. Once the plane had landed in the water, all of a sudden everything shifted to the team. Captain Sullenberger and First Officer Skiles couldn't get everybody out on their own. Everybody had to work together as a team, and once the plane was safely down in the river, people worked together as a team. Everybody raised their standards to make sure that no one was left behind. Leaders stepped up, and people functioned as a team.

Raising your standards should not only happen every day in business and in your life, but in every organization or team you're involved with—whether it's your family, job, church, or a sports team you're on. Once you raise your standards, all of a sudden you can achieve outcomes that should never have been achieved, just like what happened on the "Miracle on the Hudson." I'm forever grateful for the team I was with at Anthony Robbins. They taught me many things that helped me to help other people that day, and together we achieved an outcome that should never have been achieved.

Create Your Own Flight Plan
Exercise

1. Identify the teams you're on in your life. Examples could be your family, your church, your job, etc.

2. How do you contribute to the success of each team? How could you raise your standards and be an even better team member?

3. In which specific area of your life do you need to raise your standards? Is it your health, relationships, finances, or something else? What have you been saying you "should" do? Make a commitment to turn that "should" into a "must."

"You've got 155 people on a plane who didn't know each other, who didn't care about each other, all of a sudden pulling together to do something that has never been done before. That's one of the really key things that came out of this: when you have a mission in life and have a commonality of that mission, you can achieve anything."
–Dave Sanderson

Next Steps
Please check out my calendar at http://davesandersonspeaks.com/events. If I am in your vicinity, please contact me, and I'll send you a personal invite as my guest to the event. I'll also personalize your book!

"You can do what I cannot do.

I can do what you cannot do.

Together we can do great things."

−Mother Teresa

|12| LEADERSHIP

> "No terrible thoughts went through my head,
> none at all. I didn't worry that I might not live
> through this—and no pilot would.
> Unless the situation is completely out of your
> control, there's always something you can do."
> –First Officer Jeff Skiles

I was recently a guest on a podcast where the host asked me to talk about leadership during times of crisis. I love to talk about leadership. In fact, I have developed a program about it called Mission-Focused Leadership because of the experiences I've had and the lessons I've learned. Over the last several years I have had the opportunity to meet and talk to extraordinary people like General Norman Schwarzkopf, General Colin Powell, Supreme Court Justice Anthony Kennedy, and of course, Captain Sullenberger, as well as other leaders around the country. Every time I have the chance to talk with a leader, I ask them a certain set of questions, and one thing that I always hear is that they all had a particular mission.

What Leaders Have in Common

As I've spoken about previously, back in 1999 I had the honor of spending time with General Schwarzkopf. He disclosed that during the war he had had a singular mission, and every day he got people focused on that mission. By doing so, he was able to accomplish his mission within 60 days and win the war.

Fast forward 10 years and I had the chance to talk to Captain Sullenberger about the events of January 15, 2009. I asked him, "What was your decision-making process?" I love to hear how leaders make decisions. He responded that, once he heard the explosion, he knew that he had basically one mission: to get everybody down safely and out of the plane without sustaining injury or death.

Leadership Is Setting The Direction And Vision

That's when I realized that that's what General Schwarzkopf had also said to me, namely, to achieve his outcome, he had to focus on his mission. What I learned from both these men is that leadership is about setting the direction and the vision and letting people do what they need to do the best way they know how.

My first job out of college was in hotel and restaurant management. I knew nothing about hotel and restaurant management, but it provided a great learning ground for how to work with a team and lead different groups of people who had no common background. This experience continued for the next three years albeit in a variety of locations and with many different teams from diverse backgrounds who spoke multiple languages. These skill sets were invaluable to me in subsequent years.

Step Up or Step Back

While a member of the Tony Robbins' Security Team and later in a leadership role as the director of security, I used the skills I had learned in my first job. I also developed new skills as a leader in charge of a team of leaders. Leading leaders is a very unique skill set and is one resource I used during the evacuation of Flight 1549. On the plane that day, there were many different types of people: leaders, followers, families, and teams. When crisis hits, it is amazing how the lessons you have learned earlier in life, sometimes even 25 or 30 years prior, kick in. What I learned by being a hotel/restaurant manager and being on and leading a team of leaders suddenly became essential in helping me manage the crisis. I led when I needed to lead and checked my ego at the door, allowing others to lead when they could do the job better. And you know the rest of the story: a 100% survival rate from a commercial airplane crash in 36-degree water. It took leadership and teamwork by everybody on the plane to turn this from a potential tragedy into a miracle.

Create Your Own Flight Plan
Exercise

- What is your mission?

- What is your decision-making process in times of crisis?

- What leadership characteristics do you have? What leadership traits would you like to develop?

"Leadership is about having a vision bigger
than yourself, bigger than this moment.
Leadership is about making
your vision a reality."
–Anthony Robbins

Next Steps

Contact me at http://davesandersonspeaks.com/contact-us/ and include the word "backstory" in your message. If you do, I'll send you one video a month with the backstory of the key strategies I used to survive the "Miracle on the Hudson."

DAVE SANDERSON'S DAILY RITUALS

"You'll never change your life until
you change something you do daily.
The secret of your success is found
in your daily routine."
–John C. Maxwell

Growing a business, being a busy entrepreneur, and staying present and available for my family requires focus and discipline. Having a set routine and identifying specific outcomes are the keys to my success. Below is an example of how I structure my day.

Rituals

1. Wake up early every day so I have time to do the things that matter to me! During the school year, I wake up at 5:15 am; during the non-school year, I wake up at 5:45 am.

2. Personal hygiene always comes first.

   - When I was young, my mother always told me that someone who takes care of themselves will take care of what's important to them. Hygiene is one thing I can do to start the day to reinforce that I will take care of myself, my business, and who is important in my life.

3. Stretch out and burn calories first thing in the morning: I do a minimum of 30 minutes and up to 60 minutes of resistance training, aerobics, and now yoga on alternate days.

4. I do my "Hour of Power," which is really 30 minutes where I listen to inspirational information, music, or I say my positive affirmations.

- "Hour of Power" is a synonym for the time when you work on your mental and emotional self so you are able to be at your peak throughout the day. I commit 30 minutes to listening to positive content, affirmations, or praying until I'm ready to get on with the day. The other 30 minutes is the minimum amount of time I invest in my physical self so I will have the energy to perform

5. I go to my "money book" where I have my physical files and write down one thing I have gratitude for and thank God for opening up my mission to me.

6. I ask myself a new question every day. Some examples of the questions I ask:

- How can I add even more value to _____?

- What kind of person do I need to be today to accomplish ____?

- Who is someone I can impact today and enjoy the process?

7. I meditate for about five minutes to clear my mind.

8. When I'm home and not traveling, I see my daughter off to high school and take my son to school, as I want them to see me, and I want to give them encouragement to start their day off right.

9. I then clean up so I can start my business day.

10. When it is possible, I end my business day by 6 pm so I can have dinner with the family.

11. When I'm not traveling, I take down time in the evening and clear my mind.

12. I write down my action plan for the next day before I go through my evening rituals for my personal hygiene.

13. Before I go to bed, I either read for 15 minutes or listen to positive affirmations.

Ritual Resources

Do you have favorite products you listen to?

- Jessica Rhodes podcast, *Rhodes to Success*, opens my mind to opportunities; I have my "Last songs to go onstage," which are key songs that will gradually get me to peak state, all positive, all with different levels of energy, all with positive messages; I download on my car's hard drive Tony Robbins' CDs so I can be reinforced with strategies while I am in transit.

How do you use your phone to reinforce your goals, values, and empowering questions?

- I set reminders on my phone of what kind of person I need to be to accomplish my mission. Each one goes off on my phone as an alarm at certain times of the day. Even though I may not read them daily, the notification goes off so I know what I have committed to.

Is there anything you do monthly, quarterly, or yearly as a ritual?

- Each quarter, I reset my goal list to get in alignment with my annual goals. For example, I am behind on this year's revenue goal so I reset it and am now looking at more horizontal income.

Do you have a Sunday ritual that's unique from the rest of the week?

- Each Sunday, I go to my book (yes, paper still has a lot of value) and set up my action list for vertical income and now horizontal income, so I can focus daily on each. I also focus on administration and personal outcomes.

Do you adjust your rituals or do anything new or different when you travel?

- No, each day the notifications go up. One ritual I do when I lift weights is, before I start a set, I say my affirmations such as, "I can do all things through Christ who strengthens me," and "All power comes through Christ," and "Every day and every way I have even more _____."

Create Your Own Flight Plan
Exercise

- Create your own list of daily rituals. Start following them and notice how they impact your life.

- Put a daily reminder in your smart phone. Write down a goal you want to achieve or a reminder of the type of person you want to be. Set a daily alarm on your phone to go off and remind you of what you want.

- Schedule your quarterly goals. Block out the four dates now – one day in each quarter – for when you're going to set aside time to review your goals and set new ones.

"Days are expensive.

When you spend a day you have one less day to spend.

Make sure you spend each one wisely."

–Jim Rohn

An Exclusive Offer for *Moments Matter* Readers

Jane Blaufus, CLU is a bestselling author, keynote speaker, National TV and radio personality, and a Catalyst for Courageous Conversations. A respected 25-year veteran of the financial services industry, Jane had always thought that if the unthinkable happened, she would be well prepared and better equipped to handle the unexpected, considering her profession and expertise – wrong! One sunny Sunday, a police officer walked up her driveway and delivered the news that her thirty-nine year old husband had been killed in an accident that morning. In the blink of an eye, she became a widow with a twelve-and-a-half year old daughter and a financial tsunami coming her way.

Her book, WITH THE **[STROKE]** OF A PEN®, Claim your life, chronicles her journey in gripping detail, recounting her rise from the depth of confusion and despair while dealing with the loss of a loved one, to reclaiming her life and finding love again. Educational as well as inspirational, WITH THE **[STROKE]** OF A PEN®, Claim your life talks about the practical stuff that no one really prepares you for – or talks about. Jane wants to ensure this book is not just her story, but also a practical resource so that others can better prepare themselves to handle the unexpected, but, even more so, the inevitable. She hopes that by starting the conversation, she will help demystify the fear we have about the subject of illness and death, and our hesitation about planning for it. Jane includes a 30-page checklist at the end of the book to help people to have courageous conversations with themselves first, then with their family and offers thought provoking questions when dealing with the appropriate planning professionals.

As a companion piece to the book, Jane has also compiled one of the most comprehensive planning binders available on the market today. In it, she walks people through an easy, step-by- step process to compile all of the important personal and financial information one will need at the time of an illness or death. Both her book and planning binder have become two of the most highly recommended and sought after comprehensive and actionable pre-planning resources for families, individuals and business owners alike.

Dave Sanderson Speaks is thrilled to offer the readers of Moments Matter an opportunity to purchase these two important planning resources at an exclusive preferred price of 20 percent off each item. Simply go to the website www.theblaufusgroup.com/shop and use the Promo Code MM to make your purchase.

I know you will be thankful you will have taken advantage of this special offer when **Moments Matter** most to you.

Sincerely,

Dave

CONTRIBUTION AND GIVING BACK

**"The meaning of life is to find your gift.
The purpose of life is to give it away."
–Pablo Picasso**

As of December 2015, I have helped raise $8.1 million for the Red Cross. My goal in 2016 is to raise another $1 million. I'm donating a portion of each book sold to the Red Cross. By purchasing this book, you are contributing to the achievement of this goal.

It all began with a blanket.

I was handed a Red Cross blanket that cold January day after I was rescued from the Hudson River, and it has since become an important symbol for me. That blanket has come to represent the importance of being ready when a crisis happens. No one expects to be in a plane crash. No one expects to be in a fire, an earthquake, or any other catastrophe, but when they are, emergency response services are there, and the Red Cross is usually right behind them. I didn't open the blanket that day because I could barely move. However, I still have that blanket with me; I opened it after I got home.

When I was interviewed for a feature article in Success magazine, one of the questions they asked me was: "How did you get more involved with giving and what are your thoughts on giving?" I've been involved with The Anthony Robbins Organization for many years and have spent time with Tony personally. One of the things that he teaches at every one of his events is the power of giving and the need to contribute to others. After surviving the plane crash, I felt a strong sense of gratitude, and I wanted to figure out some way to give back. It didn't take me long to figure out exactly how I could do that. I was very fortunate and blessed to be able to build an association with the American Red Cross, not only with the chapter in my hometown of Charlotte, North Carolina, but also all over the country by helping the organization obtain much needed funds to be able to handle the disasters it responds to in local communities.

Every day, in some way, the Red Cross is out helping somebody in a crisis situation—whether it's a house fire, earthquake, tornado, flood, hurricane, or a terrorist attack. I speak at their events for free because I want to celebrate the Red Cross and help get its message out. That's why I encourage people to get involved in any way they can—give blood, donate time, and, if you have financial gifts, please share them.

The bible says that once you start contributing, it comes back tenfold; that's what happened to me. From my partnership with the Red Cross I was able to build a relationship with the luxury brand Montblanc in helping them to reach some of their philanthropic goals in the United States. Through kindness and philanthropic channels, Montblanc also donated money to the American Red Cross.

When you have the opportunity to give, take that

opportunity. You never know when or how that moment of decision to contribute is going to matter to someone else. You never know when it may directly help you or your family. And from my personal experience, knowing someone is there to help and support you during a crisis is invaluable.

Why the American Red Cross

People often ask me "Why do you donate your time to support the Red Cross?" When I speak to individuals, the backstory is usually much longer than what I share when I'm on stage.

When I was growing up in Hillsboro, Ohio, I was very active in the Boy Scouts. I loved being around a team and learning new skills. I went all-in when I became a scout. I wanted to earn all the merit badges and become an Eagle Scout. Our troop leader, Lawson Walker, was the only Eagle Scout in Hillsboro, and I wanted to be the second. The first merit badge I earned was my swimming badge. In Hillsboro, there was one public pool so all the lessons were taught there. At that time, the Red Cross was the only group giving lessons for free. That was my first interaction with the organization. I became a very proficient swimmer—to the point that I would give swimming lessons to the younger kids at the pool. The lessons I learned during the Red Cross training for my swimming merit badge paid off 41 years later when I needed to swim from a sinking plane in the Hudson River.

We lived in a neighborhood where we were surrounded by a lot of woods. The Boy Scout lodge where we met was back in those woods, along with many campsites. In the late 60s and early 70s, parents in my neighborhood sent their kids out all day without really worrying about their safety. Everyone looked out for each other; it was a much simpler time. With the lodge and campsites close to where we lived, the troop would camp out often. One night we camped out at one of the furthest points in the woods. All was going as usual—good times, telling stories, grilling hot dogs, all the things boys do. Later in the evening, one of the boys cut his hand severely as he was getting wood for the fire. It was bleeding, and we applied the first aid we were taught when we were getting our merit badges. We got the boy to his house, and his family took over from there. But that's not where the story ends. During our next meeting at the lodge, we had a Red Cross representative teach us advanced first aid training. I started to realize how important it is to know the basics and be prepared when something happens.

The Red Cross impacted my life from when I was growing up—not just from the dock in Weehawken, New Jersey. As Captain Sullenberger has said many times, when he had to glide that plane over the George Washington Bridge and land in an ice-covered river, all he did was take all those deposits of training he had and cash them in. That is what happened to me. I took all that training I had when I was young and cashed it in when I was on that plane and making my move to get out to safety. And when I got to the dock, there were three people waiting for me, two EMTs and a Red Cross volunteer.

I had three Red Cross experiences during the Miracle on the Hudson—at the dock after I was rescued, later that night at the hospital, and the next day when I arrived home to Charlotte. I became close friends with the Red Cross CEO of the Carolinas Region, Pam Jefsen. She didn't know my whole

Red Cross story when she asked me to speak at her Hero event later that year. There were over 400 people at that event, and for the first time, I shared how at each point during the rescue and after the Red Cross had impacted or influenced me. That is when I decided to learn more of what the mission of the Red Cross was really about and donate my time and efforts to the cause.

When this commitment became public, I told Red Cross senior management that my goal was to take the "Miracle" to a Red Cross in every single state so that each one could benefit. To this point, I have helped raise much-needed funds in 27 states. Some of the passengers have asked me why I do this. A couple of them seem upset that I donate my time and am getting "publicity" for what I do with the Red Cross. I believe that all of us who were on US Airways Flight 1549 have an opportunity to use our experience to help others. Captain Sullenberger has chosen to do this by donating his time to St. Jude's Children Hospital in Memphis, Tennessee. I have chosen to go all-in with the Red Cross. I have seen up-close how the organization impacts people, from being there during earthquakes, tornadoes, floods, and even the most common tragedy, house fires. Red Cross volunteers impact people every moment of every day.

- Did you know that every eight minutes the Red Cross responds to a disaster?

- Did you know that every two seconds, someone in the U.S. needs blood? The American Red Cross supplies about 40 percent of the nation's blood supply.

- Every day 20,000 people across the U.S. receive lifesaving Red Cross health and safety training, like the training I received in 1968 when I learned how to swim and the first aid training I received in 1970.

- Volunteers constitute 94 percent of the Red Cross humanitarian workforce and bring lifesaving services to communities across the country.

The Red Cross receives no money from the government; all proceeds come from people and companies like you and me. That's why I do what I do. I am honored to work with this organization. That is also why I've decided that a portion of the net proceeds from this book will go to the Red Cross. I never thought I would ever need the Red Cross, but if it wasn't for the training I received when I was young and the Red Cross volunteers present on January 15 and 16, 2009, I may not be here today.

As you put together your contribution plan going forward, find a cause that you believe in, go all-in, donate your time, and see how you can impact someone's life. You never know whose life you can change. Contribution is a spiritual need shared by all of us. It will give you fulfillment, and that is what having a joyous life is about.

ABOUT THE AMERICAN RED CROSS

The American Red Cross shelters, feeds and provides emotional support to victims of disasters; supplies about 40 percent of the nation's blood; teaches skills that save lives; provides international humanitarian aid; and supports military members and their families. The Red Cross is a not-for-profit organization that depends on volunteers and the generosity of the American public to perform its mission. For more information, please visit **redcross.org** or on Twitter at **@RedCross**.

"We make a living by what we get,

but we make a life by what we give."

−Winston Churchill

ABOUT THE AUTHORS

Dave Sanderson

Dave Sanderson is the Managing Partner of Dave Sanderson Speaks Enterprises. His thoughts on leadership have made him an internationally sought-out speaker.

Motivated by this near-death experience, the teamwork and resourcefulness demonstrated that day by him and his fellow passengers, and the compassion shown to him by rescuers, emergency professionals and concerned volunteers who looked after him, Dave has made it his life's work to give back. In the seven years since the crash, he has transitioned from a successful sales career to motivational speaking and mentoring, translating the Miracle on the Hudson into an inspirational message that resonates far beyond what happened that day, and which he hopes will be relevant to everyone in his audience.

In addition to speaking and training, Dave conducts workshops and shares the story of Flight 1549, revealing the inner strength it took to make it through the day, and how teamwork, leadership, and state management can help overcome any obstacle.

He and his wife, Terri, reside in Charlotte, North Carolina with their four children.

www.davesandersonspeaks.com

Cindy Wrightson

Cindy Wrightson has established herself as an expert in content development working with speakers, authors, entrepreneurs, and corporations to create, develop, and write content for multi-media products. Prior to launching her content consulting firm, Cindy served as Content Development Manager for Robbins Research International, Inc. (an Anthony Robbins Company). For more than a decade she collaborated on content for Mr. Robbins' live events, television appearances, high-profile meetings, and multi-media products. She resides in San Diego, California. For inquiries, cindywrightson@gmail.com

www.cindywrightson.com

CBS *Up to the Minute* (2014): On the 5-year anniversary of the "Miracle on the Hudson" I was on evening 2 of 3 of filming a piece for the *CBS Evening News with Scott Pelley*. The producer from the overnight show *Up to the Minute* heard I was in town and at 7pm on January 12, 2014 I received a call asking me if I would go on with Anne-Marie Green. I arrived at CBS headquarters in New York City about midnight to get prepared to go on with Anne-Marie. We did a 10-minute live interview about the "Miracle" and the path I took after the crash. The piece aired all through the night and she was kind to take this picture with me!

Geraldo Rivera (2009): I was in New York City getting ready to be on *Good Morning America* and the *Early Show*. I arrived in NYC on Sunday afternoon and received a call from Geraldo's show producers asking me if I was in town and if I would be open to be on his show that night. It was good timing.

Captain Sully (2014): on the 5-year anniversary of the "Miracle on the Hudson," CBS did a piece on my family and me. They started in Charlotte then followed me to New York City then to New Jersey. When I got to New York, as I was going into the studio to do a piece, Captain Sullenberger was going in to film a story as the Aviation Consultant. This was the first time seeing him in over a year

My family (2012): Together at the high school graduation of Colleen

Tony Robbins (1999): after traveling with Tony for the year, this was his last Competitive Edge event ever. He grabbed me and thanked me for being there with him

Now What?

Let's stay connected! For more behind the scenes content, bonuses, videos, and updates, register this book at:

www.momentsmatterbook.com

"A happy life is just a string of happy moments. But most people don't allow the happy moment, because they're so busy trying to get a happy life."

–Abraham-Hicks